THIS IS HISTORY!

The Twentieth Century

A WORLD STUDY SINCE 1900

CHRISTOPHER CULPIN

Hodder Murray

A MEMBER OF THE HODDER HEADLINE GROUP

The Schools History Project

The Project was set up in 1972, with the aim of improving the study of History for students aged 13–16. This involved a reconsideration of the ways in which History contributes to the educational needs of young people. The Project devised new objectives, new criteria for planning and developing courses, and the materials to support them. New examinations, requiring new methods of assessment, also had to be developed. These have continued to be popular. The advent of GCSE in 1987 led to the expansion of Project approaches into other syllabuses.

The Schools History Project has been based at Trinity and All Saints College, Leeds, since 1978, from where it supports teachers through a biennial Bulletin, regular INSET, an annual Conference and a website (www.tasc.ac.uk/shp).

Since the National Curriculum was drawn up in 1991, the Project has continued to expand its publications, bringing its ideas to courses for Key Stage 3 as well as a range of GCSE and A level specifications.

Note: The wording and sentence structure of some written sources have been adapted and simplified to make them accessible to all pupils, while faithfully preserving the sense of the original.

Words printed in SMALL CAPITALS are defined in the glossary on page 92.

Orders: please contact Bookpoint Ltd, 130 Milton Park, Abingdon, Oxon OX14 4SB. Telephone: +44 (0)1235 827720. Fax: +44 (0)1235 400454. Lines are open from 9.00 to 5.00, Monday to Saturday, with a 24-hour message answering service. You can also visit our websites www.hodderheadline.co.uk and www.hoddersamplepages.co.uk

First published in 2004
by Hodder Murray, an imprint of Hodder Education, a member of the Hodder Headline Group
338 Euston Road
London NW1 3BH

Reprinted 2005, 2006

Layouts by Amanda Hawkes
Artwork by Art Construction, Peter Bull, Jon Davis/Linden Artists, Richard Duszczak, Oxford Designers and Illustrators, Tony Randell, Steve Smith, Craig Warwick/Linden Artists
Typeset in 13/15pt Goudy by Phoenix Photosetting, Chatham, Kent
Printed and bound in Italy

A catalogue entry for this book is available from the British Library

Pupil's Book ISBN-10: 0 7195 7711 X
ISBN-13: 978 0 7195 7711 6
Teacher's Resource Book ISBN-10: 0 7195 7712 8
ISBN-13: 978 0 7195 7712 3

◆ Contents

INTRODUCTION: 'NOW THAT'S WHAT I CALL IMPORTANT ...!'

Think about what makes something significant

◆ Significant events ... in British history

Of all the things you have ever learned about in History, which do you think really ought to be taught? Which are the most **significant**?

ACTIVITY A

1 Work in small groups to list events that you have studied in History in Years 7, 8 and 9. Think of as many as you can. Write each event on a separate card. These pictures may give you some ideas to start with.

2 Still in groups or as a whole class place the event cards on a line from 'most significant event' to 'least significant event'.

3 Choose your 'most' and your 'least' significant event and write down as many reasons as you can *why* the most significant is more significant than the least significant.

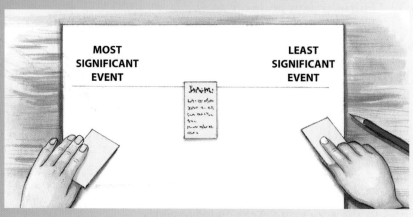

MOST SIGNIFICANT EVENT

LEAST SIGNIFICANT EVENT

◆ *Significant events ... in the twentieth century*

Here are twenty things that happened in the twentieth century. You may know about some of them already.

1 Human beings landed on the moon for the first time

2 Six million Jews and others were killed by the Nazis in Germany

3 Britain and its allies defeated Germany and its allies in the Second World War

4 Black athlete Jesse Owens won a record four gold medals at the Berlin Olympic Games in 1936

5 David Beckham was sent off for kicking an Argentinian opponent in the World Cup of 1998

6 American President John F. Kennedy was ASSASSINATED by Lee Harvey Oswald

7 Roger Bannister ran the first ever sub-four-minute mile

8 Bill Gates founded a computer software company called Microsoft

9 India became independent from Britain

10 The first atom bomb was dropped on Hiroshima killing 80,000 people

11 Adolf Hitler, leader of Nazi Germany, killed himself in a bunker in Berlin

12 The first ever Tesco supermarket opened in 1929 in Burnt Oak, Edgware

13 Christopher Culpin (author of this book) was born

14 Concorde flew from Britain to America in a record-beating 150 minutes

15 Captain Scott became the first Briton to reach the South Pole. He died on the return journey

16 South Africa introduced APARTHEID, making black people second class citizens

17 Around 9 million soldiers were killed in the Great War

18 Chris Wells – son of Jane and Paul Wells – took his first steps at the age of 13 months

19 Ernest Chain helped discover the first ANTIBIOTIC – penicillin

20 British women were allowed to vote in a general election for the first time

ACTIVITY B

1 Place each of the above events on a line from 'most significant event' to 'least significant event'. **Note: there is no right answer.** It is up to you to decide on the significance of the events.

2 If you are going to decide which new trainers to buy, you use *criteria*. For example: Will I look good in them? Are they fashionable? What will my friends say about them? Do they do the job I want them for? Can I afford them? (Perhaps even: what will my parents say about them?) In the same way, people have **criteria** for deciding the significance of events in history.

Choose two of your 'most' and two of your 'least' significant events and write down as many reasons as you can think of *why* you put them there. These reasons are your **criteria**.

◆ Welcome to Significance Alley

When the British government decided what history topics young people should study at school they were very specific about the twentieth century:

- ◆ the First World War
- ◆ the Second World War
- ◆ the Cold War
- ◆ the Holocaust.

They thought that these events were so significant that every pupil in every school should study them! So two big questions for this book are:

1 Why are these events so significant?
2 Do you agree that they are significant?

To help you decide you will be visiting Significance Alley.

THINK ABOUT SIGNIFICANCE

1 CRITERION 1: people at the time thought it was important

2 CRITERION 2: it affected a lot of people

3 CRITERION it affected people deeply

4 CRITERION 4: it affected people for a long time

5 CRITERION 5: it still affects attitudes or beliefs today

6 CRITERION 6: it led to other important events

As you study different events in the twentieth century you will think about which of these 'criterion' skittles the event knocks over. A really significant event will knock over more skittles than a less significant one.

DISCUSS

Look back to your criteria for significance from the activities on pages 2–3. Compare your criteria with those we have shown in Significance Alley. Are yours the same or different?

WHAT WAS SO 'GREAT' ABOUT THE GREAT WAR?

The Great War is simply another name for the First World War 1914–18. People only started calling it the *First* World War after the *Second* World War broke out in 1939. To people at the time it was 'the Great War' because it was the biggest war in history. It lasted more than four years. There was fighting in at least ten countries as well as at sea. The Great War would still be on most people's list of events in the twentieth century that should be remembered. Why?

The Great War was 'great' because …

lots of countries got involved

millions of soldiers were killed

everyone, including civilians, was affected

it changed attitudes to war

In this section you will think about these and other reasons why the Great War was significant.

Harry Bell

This is Harry Bell. He was born in 1900 and lives in West Hartlepool in north-east England. He is 14 years old. He left school two years ago, and now works as an APPRENTICE shipbuilder. One of his hobbies is building model ships.

Harry is poor but he lives in one of the richest countries in the world. Britain has a vast EMPIRE that spreads across the world. It is the largest empire the world has ever known. The empire is the area marked in pink on the map on Harry's wall. Look closely round Harry's room and compare his life with yours.

3 OPPORTUNITY: Harry went to school from age five but left when he was twelve. He liked school. He is good at reading, but he did not need to stay on at school because he knew he was always going to be a shipbuilder and young apprentices like Harry start training at age twelve. He expects to stay in this job all his life just like his father has done.

2 HEALTH: Harry's LIFE EXPECTANCY is about 61 – this is better than his father, although there are several diseases for which there are still no cures. Even a flu EPIDEMIC can kill thousands of people.

1 TRAVEL: In 1914 you can get across the oceans of the world in a steamship like Harry's model. The USA is at least eight days away from Europe; Australia is ten weeks away. Travel on land is slow, even impossible in some parts of Britain. There are only a few hundred cars in existence and there is a 3mph speed limit. There are no traffic jams. Harry does not know anyone who owns a car. Human beings have only just begun to fly short distances, using powered aeroplanes.

THIS IS TO CERTIFY THAT HARRY BELL

4 WAR: There are wars, of course. Harry's oldest brother fought in the most recent war Britain was involved in – the Boer War, or South African War, 1899–1903. But it had seemed very far away. Civilians read about the war and sometimes they mourned a death or celebrated a victory, but mostly they got on with their lives in complete safety. There was no way the Boers could have attacked Britain. Britain has not been successfully invaded by a foreign army for over 800 years.

ACTIVITY

I Compare your life with Harry's. You could use a chart like this (we have started the first row for you). For each row think about your own room; or your own family's daily life. For example: for trade, think about where your clothes, shoes, food, phone, games, electronic equipment, etc are made.

Theme	Harry's world	My world
Travel	Not much. International travel was by sea	A lot. International travel is by air
Health		
Opportunity		
War		
Trade		
Information		

Research challenge

2 We have told you quite a lot about Harry's world but not everything. What other questions have you got about Harry's world?
  a) Write down your questions on separate pieces of paper.
  b) Pick one out at random.
  c) See how much information you can research to answer that question *in just 15 minutes*.

6 INFORMATION: Newspapers are the only way of finding out what is going on in the outside world. Radio and the telephone have only just been invented, so news travels slowly. Many people live their entire lives without knowing anything about what is happening outside the area where they live. There is no TV, no internet, no mobile phones.

DISCUSS

What do you think is the worst thing that could happen to Harry? Work with a partner and discuss possible ingredients of a short story in which disaster comes to Harry Bell. What might happen to him?

5 TRADE: There is some world-wide trade, carried out by rich European countries and the USA, but everything in Harry's room comes from Britain, except: the bed is made from African wood; the brass ornament was made in India; and the toy comes from Germany.

◆ *How was Harry Bell's world shattered?*

It was early on the morning of 16 December 1914. Harry was already at work.

SOURCE 2 Moor Terrace, Hartlepool, after the attack.

SOURCE 1

I was working at Gray's Central Shipyard. I had just finished warming my can of tea, at about 8.20a.m., when gunfire could be heard and everybody went out to see what was happening. In a few seconds a shell hit the office and blew nearly all of it into the air and at the same time railway wagons were being blown sky-high. Men who were running in that direction turned and made their way towards the back gate leading to Slag Island Quay. Nearing this gate I climbed on one of the uprights and saw that the gasometers were on fire and shouted down to the men who were running towards the gate what I could see. They all yelled at me 'Get down, you young ...!', so I did. The shells were coming thick and fast but luckily quite a lot fell in the timber-ponds.

Reaching the corner of Middleton Road and Hartlepool Road I noticed a young boy stretched over the tramlines face downwards and when I went over to him I saw that he was dead with nearly all his chest blown away. A few yards further I saw Barney Hodgson pinned against the church wall and bleeding very badly. I ran towards him and he said 'Keep running, son, I'm done for'.

When I reached home my mother was propped up against the wall of our house with blood running from her like water from a tap and in the road opposite was a boy by the name of Joseph Jacobs who was dead. I ran to the bottom of our street and took a barrow from the yard and ran back with it to our house to put my mother on it to take her to hospital. It was then that my brother Tom came up and between us we got my mother and the boy Jacobs on to the cart. Later we stopped a coal cart and asked the driver to take them to hospital, which he did.

At the mortuary I identified my youngest brother who had been killed. Another brother was in hospital with leg injuries. Our family's total casualties were my mother – a lost leg and multiple injuries, a brother killed, a brother with leg injuries and a nephew killed.

In total, 127 people in Hartlepool, including men, women and children, died in the space of 45 minutes that grey morning. They were killed by shells fired from three German battle-cruisers that had come in close to the shore. More were killed when Whitby and Scarborough were shelled later that day. These people were the first civilians to be killed in Britain in the Great War. They were not to be the last.

Nowadays we almost take it for granted that civilians are targeted when there is a war. In 1914 this was a new idea. This was the first war in which civilians became the deliberate targets of enemy guns.

The continuing story of Harry Bell

We don't know what happened to Harry next. Maybe, like thousands of young men, he joined the army and fought in the trenches on the Western Front. Maybe he stayed on working at the shipyard, building the battleships that helped to bring eventual victory to the Allies. We do know he was still alive in 1964, which is when someone went to interview him and record his memories of December 1914. Unfortunately the interviewer either did not ask about or did not write down the story of the rest of Harry's life. Maybe he or she did not think that those other things were important. History is often like that. We only know about the bits that someone else thought were significant enough to write down.

ACTIVITY A

You are a reporter on the Hartlepool local newspaper. Rough out the front page of your newspaper for the day after the attack. Include:

a) a headline
b) a caption for the photo (Source 2)
c) some quotes from eye-witnesses (based on Source 1)
d) an explanation of what weapons caused this damage
e) your explanation of why these attacks were made on ordinary British people.

ACTIVITY B

This is Significance Alley. Over the next 12 pages you will be gathering evidence to show why the Great War was significant. You will see which of these skittles the Great War knocks down: is it a 'strike', knocking down all six skittles? If it is, then the Great War would be very significant indeed.

Start with Harry Bell. There is certainly plenty in Harry's story to show that the Great War was significant for him.

1 How would Harry finish this sentence: 'The Great War was significant because ...'?
2 Which criterion skittle do your answers to question 1 relate to?
Discuss
3 Do you think ordinary people like Harry matter in history? Is it worth studying them?
4 Your story: many families have members who were personally affected by the Great War, just like Harry. Try to find out if anything happened to any of your grandparents, great grandparents or other relatives.

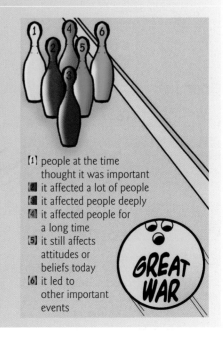

[1] people at the time thought it was important
[2] it affected a lot of people
[3] it affected people deeply
[4] it affected people for a long time
[5] it still affects attitudes or beliefs today
[6] it led to other important events

WHY DID THE GREAT WAR HAPPEN?
... and were the Alliances most to blame?

Most of the wars you will have studied in history were fought between just two countries. The Great War was different. All the most powerful countries in the world were dragged in. How did this happen?

◆ Forty _years_ up to the Great War

For many years tension had been building in Europe. This diagram shows the main reasons.

Patriotism People were deeply patriotic. They wanted their own country to be the best and most successful.

Rival empires Each European power had an overseas empire. Britain had the biggest. Germany wanted more.

The ARMS RACE Germany and Russia were building up massive armies. Germany and Britain were building lots of new warships.

Alliances Countries made ALLIANCES with each other (see map). They promised to protect the other members of the alliance if they were attacked.

Key
Central powers
Entente powers

BRITAIN
GERMANY RUSSIA
FRANCE
AUSTRIA-HUNGARY
Sarajevo
SERBIA
ITALY
N
0 500 km

TENSIONS IN EUROPE

PATRIOTISM · RIVAL EMPIRES · THE ARMS RACE · ALLIANCES · WAR PLANS · THE KAISER

War plans War was accepted as a way for countries to get what they wanted. Some people wanted a war. Others said there was 'bound to be a war sometime'. Some were making careful plans for how to win a war if and when it happened.

The Kaiser For forty years Germany had been growing stronger. Germany's enemies were suspicious of the German ruler – called the Kaiser. They thought he wanted to make Germany stronger still.

U16143

◆ *Forty <u>days</u> up to the Great War*

ACTIVITY A

1 The reasons on page 10 are all connected. For example, countries made *alliances* because they were worried about the *arms race*.

Draw, label and cut out six sticks of dynamite for yourself. Put them on a large blank sheet of paper. Work with a partner to see how many connections you can make. Draw lines to show these links. Write on each line what the link is.

2 Write a paragraph to explain why the alliance system could turn a small local conflict into a much bigger one. Try to use some of the other dynamite sticks in your explanation.

In June 1914 Sarajevo in Bosnia suddenly became very important to the whole future of Europe.

Bosnia belonged to Austria–Hungary, but the people of Serbia felt that it should belong to them. On Sunday, 28 June 1914, Archduke Franz Ferdinand (son of the Emperor of Austria–Hungary) and his wife Sophie visited Sarajevo. It was a dangerous thing to do. The Archduke knew there were people in Sarajevo who hated Austria–Hungary.

At 10.45a.m. Franz Ferdinand and Sophie were shot dead by a Serb student. Five weeks later all the great powers of Europe were at war. This is how it happened.

28 June Archduke murdered

5 July Germany promises to support Austria–Hungary if it attacks Serbia

23 July Austria–Hungary blames Serbia for the murder

29 July Russia prepares its army for war to help its ally, Serbia

28 July Austria–Hungary declares war on Serbia

1 August Germany declares war on Russia

2 August France prepares army for war

3 August Germany declares war on France and invades Belgium

4 August Britain declares war on Germany

DISCUSS

Is there any one event on this page which, if you took it away, would mean the war would not have happened? Give reasons.

11

The timeline and Sources 1–7 give an overview of the Great War.

SOURCE 2 British forces, with many Australians and New Zealanders (ANZACS), landed at Gallipoli to defeat Germany's ally, Turkey. The expedition failed, with heavy losses.

SOURCE 1 The generals expected a short, fast-moving war. Germany invaded France rapidly in August 1914 but failed (just) to capture Paris. Both sides settled into trenches which, by the end of 1914, stretched from Switzerland to the English Channel.

SOURCE 3 Both Britain and Germany had huge navies but the only time they met was at the Battle of Jutland. The battle ended in a draw, but the British navy was still able to prevent important overseas supplies such as petrol and food from reaching Germany. In the end this led to the German defeat.

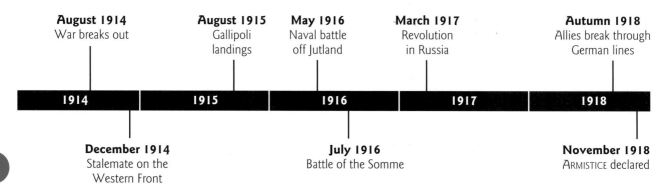

August 1914
War breaks out

August 1915
Gallipoli landings

May 1916
Naval battle off Jutland

March 1917
Revolution in Russia

Autumn 1918
Allies break through German lines

| 1914 | 1915 | 1916 | 1917 | 1918 |

December 1914
Stalemate on the Western Front

July 1916
Battle of the Somme

November 1918
ARMISTICE declared

SOURCE 6 At the end of the war the town of Ypres in France, which had a population of 20,000 before the war, was a ghost town with hardly a building left undamaged. The human cost of the war was even higher, as the table in Source 7 shows.

SOURCE 4 The huge Russian army was badly led and badly supplied. By 1917 thousands of Russians had died on the Eastern Front. This led to the overthrow of the country's leader, the Tsar, in the revolution of March 1917. In November 1917 a COMMUNIST government took over Russia and took the country, now the USSR, out of the war.

Soldiers killed in the Great War	
Germany	1,950,000
Russia	1,700,000
France (and French empire)	1,500,000
Austria	1,050,000
Britain (and British empire)	1,000,000
Italy	533,000
USA	116,000

SOURCE 7 Casualties of the Great War.

SOURCE 5

There was a last, and nearly successful, German attack on the Western Front in spring 1918. After it failed, the Allies with support from newly-arrived US troops and better use of new technology, such as tanks, began to push back the German forces. An armistice was agreed on 11 November 1918.

ACTIVITY

Using your own research see if you can find a suitable picture to use as Source 2 or Source 5. Your teacher can give you some suggestions about where to look, or you could use the internet, the library or look in other textbooks. Write a couple of sentences to explain each choice.

◆ *How was this war different?*

One thing most people know about the Great War is that it was the first time soldiers had fought in trenches. Here you will find out why.

Source 8 shows trenches on the Western Front. From late 1914 to mid-1918 troops were stuck in these trenches.

Why did the two sides get bogged down in this way? As we shall see later in this book, other twentieth century wars had lots of movement. But the particular stage that warfare technology had reached in the period 1914–18 meant that this was to be static war, fought in trenches: a war of *stalemate*.

There was stalemate because the sides were so evenly matched.

◆ Each had huge armies – millions of men.

◆ Each had modern transport – such as railway trains – to get these millions of men to the battlefront.

◆ Each had modern factories to supply them with millions of guns, shells and bullets.

Neither side could advance. So they dug themselves into trenches which were easy to defend. The trenches were home. For days at a time soldiers lived, ate and slept in them.

The two sides attacked each other by going 'over the top' – climbing up and over the trench wall and then running towards the enemy line to try to capture it. Two nineteenth century inventions made this very hard (and very dangerous) however. Barbed wire slowed down the charging soldiers, while the machine guns the enemy were using could fire 200 bullets a minute to mow them down. The casualties from this kind of attack were horrific.

On the first day of the Battle of the Somme (1 July 1916), 21,000 British soldiers were killed, mostly by enemy machine gun fire. It was a similar story on the Eastern Front where the German armies were fighting the Russians.

SOURCE 8 An artist's impression of the trenches on the Western Front.

Front line trenches – just a few hundred metres from the enemy front line

No Man's Land

Barbed wire barriers

SNIPER

Communication trenches

Big guns behind the lines

SOURCE 9 Corporal W.H. Shaw was in the Royal Welch Fusiliers at the Battle of the Somme, 1916.

There is a saying in the Royal Welch Fusiliers: 'Follow the flash'. Now I don't know if you've ever seen a Royal Welch Fusiliers officer, but there's a flash on the back of his collar. The officers were urging us on, saying 'Come on lads, follow the flash'. But you just couldn't. It was hopeless. And those young officers going ahead, that flash flying in the breeze, they were picked off like flies. We tried to go over and it was impossible. We were mown down and that went on and if some of the BATTALION did manage to break through, it was very rare and it was only on a small scale. If they did, the Germans would counter-attack and that's what was going on.

When they were counter-attacking, well, they were mown down, just the same as what we were, and yet they were urged on by their officers just the same as our officers were urging us on. They were coming over just like cattle, whole battalions of them. You just felt: 'You've given it to us, now we're going to give it to you' and you were taking a delight in mowing them down. Our machine-gunners had a whale of a time with those Lewis machine-guns. You just couldn't miss.'

Each side also had massive guns which pounded the enemy trenches with shells, trying to destroy their dugouts or kill their soldiers. In the trenches more soldiers were killed by shells than by any other cause including machine guns or disease.

By the time the battlefields had been trenched, shelled and fought over for a while the scene looked like Source 10. The flat land of northern France and Belgium, which was the part of the line held by British troops, soon became a muddy chaos, in which no buildings, trees or other living thing survived above ground.

SOURCE 10 *The Harvest of Battle*, painted in 1919 by C.R.W. Nevinson.

WHAT HAPPENED ON THE HOME FRONT?

…and how did the Great War become a 'total war'?

David Lloyd George was the British Prime Minister in 1916. He said: 'A soldier cannot function without the farms, the factory-workers and all the other providers behind them. Nowadays there is no such thing in a war as a non-combatant.'

He meant that this war involved everyone. The country was more important than individuals. This was **total war**.

◆ Recruitment

Britain had only a small army in 1914. After just a few weeks of war it was clear that it wasn't enough. For the time being, the Indian army was rushed to fight in France but it was clear that a large British army would be needed.

A huge campaign was launched to persuade young men to join up, led by the army hero Lord Kitchener. The campaign was based on:

◆ patriotism: love of your country and your duty to fight for it
◆ heroism: sharing in the glory of a great victory
◆ anti-German hatred: they spread propaganda stories of atrocities against babies by German soldiers
◆ shame: women handed out white feathers (a symbol of cowardice) to young men not in uniform.

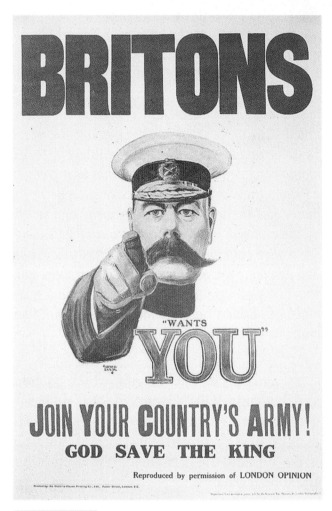

SOURCE 2 This poster features Lord Kitchener. It became one of the most famous posters of the whole war.

SOURCE 1 Some women signed this declaration:

At this hour of England's peril, I do hereby pledge myself most solemnly in the name of my King and Country to persuade every man I know to offer his services to his country. I also pledge myself never to be seen in public with any man who, being in every way fit and free for service, has refused to respond to his country's call.

The recruitment campaign was very successful: between August 1914 and December 1915 nearly 2 million men enlisted, 300,000 in the first month. In some communities almost all the young men joined up. You can imagine the impact it would have on your local area if all the young men suddenly left to go to war. This was the largest British army ever assembled. There were more civilians learning to be soldiers than ever before in history.

SOURCE 3 In some areas whole groups of friends signed on together and became a 'Pals regiment'. These are some of the Accrington Pals.

SOURCE 4 From the *Yorkshire Post*, September 1914.

Stirring scenes were witnessed at Leeds City Football ground last night at the end of the match. The Lord Mayor addressed a crowd of 4000 spectators. There was a spirited rush across the field and rousing cheers. Up the steps sturdy young fellows came, to receive an armlet with the national colours. When the rush subsided, it was found that the number of volunteers was 149. The Lady Mayoress called for another 51. Another dash was made and, to the chorus of 'It's a Long Way to Tipperary!', the quota was quickly filled.

SOURCE 5 Some young men joined up even though they were too young or too small. Charlie Taylor went to sign up with his pals:

They asked me my height and I told them. They hummed and haaed about it. I'm five foot six [167cm] with paper stuffed into my shoes. Anyway I says to them: 'There's six of my pals joining up, all footballers.' So they says, 'Aw, go on, let him go in.' So I was one of the midgets.

Everyone wanted to be involved. They did not want to miss out on the event of the century. And it was a similar story all over Europe ...

SOURCE 6 A young Frenchman wrote home:

Thirty years of life would not be worth all that we are going to achieve within the next few weeks. I wish you could share in some way the peace we all feel here.

SOURCE 7 A young German soldier wrote home as he prepared to go to the Front:

At last we have got our orders. Dear Mother, please try to remember that, if at this time we think of ourselves and those who belong to us, we shall be petty and weak. We must have a broad outlook and think of our nation, our Fatherland, and God.'

SOURCE 8 A young British officer wrote home:

You must all keep cheerful for my sake and it will not be long before I am back again. The general view is that it will not be a long show.

These were not desperate people, born losers, but keen and optimistic men. This extract from a popular school reading-book of the time might help to explain their actions.

SOURCE 9 From *The Hill*, by H.A. Vachell, published in 1905.

To die young, clean ... to die swiftly, in perfect health; to die saving others from death, or worse, disgrace; ... to die and to carry with you into the better life beyond the grave, hopes and ambitions, unembittered memories, all the freshness and gladness of May – is that not a cause for joy rather than sorrow?

A C T I V I T Y

You are a reporter at the event described in Source 4. You interview one of the 200 young men who have just volunteered to join the army.
a) What questions might you ask him?
b) What answers might he give?
Use the sources on these two pages to give you ideas.

D I S C U S S

1 Read through Sources 5–8. What is the attitude of the young man in each case? What does he expect the war to be like?
2 The men in Sources 5–8 come from three different countries. What attitudes do they have in common?
3 Read Source 9. These attitudes are not heard today. Why not?

◆ Conscription

By the end of 1915 the supply of volunteers was not enough to replace the soldiers being killed or injured, so in January 1916 the government introduced CONSCRIPTION. Every unmarried male between the ages of 18 and 41 *had* to join up. In April 1916 married men in the same age-group were added.

◆ Conscientious objectors

The government believed Britain was fighting for its life. It believed it therefore had the right to force people to fight, and if necessary to kill, for Britain. Most people in Britain agreed it had that right. But some disagreed. Their *consciences* would not let them kill other people and so they *objected*. They were therefore called conscientious objectors (or COs).

There were about 14,000 conscientious objectors. Three-quarters of them were SOCIALISTS. They said the war was controlled by bosses, industrialists, bankers, kings and rulers. The COs said they had no quarrel with workers in Germany and other countries, who were suffering just as much as workers in Britain.

SOURCE 10 The Independent Labour Party proclaimed in August 1914:

Out of the darkness we hail our working class comrades of every land. Across the roar of guns we send greetings to German socialists – they are no enemies of ours, but faithful friends. In forcing this appalling crisis upon the nations it is the rulers, the diplomats, the militarists who have sealed their doom.

Long Live Freedom and Fraternity! Long Live International Socialism!

The remainder of the conscientious objectors had religious motives. They were Christian pacifists, like the Quakers, who took seriously the sixth of the Ten Commandments: 'Thou shalt not kill'.

What happened to conscientious objectors?

The law was quite clear: if you had a genuine conscientious objection to fighting then you could be excused entirely from military service and given non-military work such as farming, mining or ambulance driving. A group of local people, a tribunal, met to decide if you were genuine. Unfortunately, many of the tribunals were BIASED against COs. Many tribunals were made up of army officers.

SOURCE 11 The chairman of the Wirral tribunal, Merseyside, speaking in 1916:

I wish the government had not put in this clause about conscientious objectors. I don't agree with it myself.

SOURCE 12 The words of a councillor at Shaw, Manchester, serving on a tribunal in 1916:

I think you are exploiting God to save your own skin. A man who would not help to defend his own country and womenkind is a coward. You are nothing but a shivering mass of unwholesome fat.

Of the 14,000 conscientious objectors who came before the tribunals:

◆ 400 received total exemption
◆ 6000 were sent to do 'work of national importance'
◆ 5000 were given non-fighting duties in the army
◆ 2600 had their cases rejected completely and were told they had to join the army as regular soldiers.

Half of the 2600 refused to do so. That was when trouble really started. Most were arrested. They were taken to an army barracks and ordered to put on uniform. Again, most refused. They were now disobeying military orders, for which the punishments were severe. Thirty COs were sent to join the army in France. They were now on 'active service', so could be shot for disobeying orders.

Gradually the army realised that they were wasting their time with these men. They could not force someone to change their attitude, and an uncommitted soldier was not much use to the army. Dealing with the COs also used up valuable resources – soldiers were taken away from their main duties in order to guard COs, and punish them. From 1916, COs who refused to cooperate were sentenced instead to prison with hard labour. After the war they lost the right to vote for five years.

These punishments may seem bizarre, but Britain was in the grip of a terrible war. In 1916, there were 400,000 British casualties in the Battle of the Somme alone. Many people found it hard to understand why some men were unwilling to 'do their bit' for their country.

ACTIVITY

How would you deal with conscientious objectors?

Do you think the government has the right to force someone to fight?

You have been asked to help draw up advice for the government to help them deal with COs. Your advice should be presented in three sections:

◆ How can you tell whether someone is a genuine CO and not just a coward?

◆ Who should decide?

◆ What do you do with genuine COs: punish them; make them work; set them free to do whatever they want?

SOURCE 13   Hubert Peet was arrested for refusing military service in 1916. He was imprisoned three times. On one occasion, he recorded:

We were marched into the middle of a large open area, used as a parade-ground. Then various groups of soldiers appeared until there must have been several thousand of them. Then the adjutant [officer] read out the charge: Private _____ tried by field court-martial for disobedience. Sentenced to death by being shot. (Pause) Confirmed by General Sir Douglas Haig (longer pause) and commuted [reduced] to ten years' hard labour.

SOURCE 14   These COs were sent to work in a quarry on Dartmoor, 1916.

SOURCE 15   This cartoon was printed in the patriotic magazine *John Bull* in 1918.

◆ Industry

It was soon clear to the leaders of each of the countries taking part in the Great War that they needed not only lots of soldiers, but also large amounts of weapons and ammunition.

So, industry was going to be as important as soldiers or generals in winning this war.

New factories were quickly built. For example, in 1915 a site at Barnbow, near Leeds had no electricity, gas, water, road or rail links; a year later there was a huge new munitions factory there, turning out 6000 shells a day.

All these new factories needed new workers – where would they come from? Most of the men had been taken into the army!

◆ Women workers

Before the war women and men did different jobs. Most well-paid, powerful jobs were open only to men. Women were usually expected to take low-paid jobs as servants, secretaries or shop assistants. Some unmarried women did work in factories, but they did the least skilled work, and they were paid less than men. Women were expected to stop working when they got married.

Total war meant changing this attitude to women workers. Male workers had joined the army so women were taken on to fill their jobs. In 1914 there had been no women at all working at Woolwich Arsenal, a munitions factory in London; by 1917 there were 25,000.

SOURCE 16 Lottie Wiggins described her work at Woolwich Arsenal:

In April 1916, Polly and myself decided we would get a job on munitions. I was only seventeen but I was taken on. Along with eight other girls we were taken to the Store and told we were going to be trained to drive the overhead cranes. We could hardly believe our eyes. We had to climb up a ladder to the crane and get down by means of a rope. I was never very brave, but this took the cake. But if I failed to mount the ladder, I was out of a job, so up I went.

My first impression was sheer fright: rows and rows of shells, including the 12-inch [30cm], which reached higher than my waist. I hardly dared walk near them, but had to overcome this feeling.

We were on eight-hour shifts at first but this was changed to twelve hours. No one would work these hours today, but there was a war on.

SOURCE 17 A woman working in Woolwich Arsenal.

SOURCE 18 Women resurfacing a road in London.

There were similar changes in other industries as well. Only 9000 women worked for the railways in 1914; by 1917 there were 50,000 women railway workers. And 30,000 women became agricultural labourers with the Women's Land Army.

Women workers showed that the old ideas about what they were capable of were nonsense. Many proved that, given the chance, they could learn the skills and do virtually all the work any man could do. However, attitudes do not change overnight, as you can see from Sources 19 and 20.

SOURCE 19 Dorothy Poole worked alongside men in an engineering works:

Over and over again the foreman gave me wrong or incomplete instructions or altered them in such a way as to make me work more hours. None of the men spoke to me for a long time and would give me no help as to where to find things. My drawer was nailed up by the men, and oil was poured over everything in it through a crack one night.

Even the women who got nearest to the fighting, the WAAC (Women's Auxiliary Army Corps), some of whom were killed by enemy guns, were only given jobs as secretaries, cleaners, clerks or cooks. The VAD (Voluntary Aid Detachment) nurses in France were working at the FRONT LINE, but they were simply carrying out another traditional role for women in wartime.

Once the war was over, most women workers were laid off almost immediately.

SOURCE 20 In 1918, the *Southampton Times* insisted that:

There is no reason to feel sympathetic towards the young woman who has been earning 'pin money' while the men have been fighting. Women who left domestic service to enter a factory are now required to return to their pots and pans.

By 1921 only 31 per cent of all women were working; in 1911 there had been 32 per cent.

However, one unexpected outcome of the changing role of women during the war was the right to vote. Before the war no women had been allowed to vote. But many people who had been opposed to giving women the vote changed their mind during the war. In 1918, shortly before the war ended, women aged over 30 were given the right to vote.

ACTIVITY

'Women's lives were totally changed by the war.' Write a response to this statement explaining whether it is accurate. Plan your answer like this:

1 Select sources and information to show that women's lives were deeply changed by the war. Make a list or a spider diagram to explain your findings.

2 Select sources and information to show that the war made little difference to women. Make another list or diagram.

3 Now write up your response to the big question, with one paragraph based on each list and a third paragraph giving your conclusion.

REVIEW ACTIVITY A

Was the Great War significant?

We're back at Significance Alley. Remember each of the skittles is a criterion for significance. Your task is to use what you have found out about the Great War to see which skittles it knocks down. In order for the Great War to knock down a skittle you will need to show evidence that the Great War meets this criterion. You can do this using the stages set out below.

[1] people at the time thought it was important
[2] it affected a lot of people
[3] it affected people deeply
[4] it affected people for a long time
[5] it still affects attitudes or beliefs today
[6] it led to other important events

GREAT WAR

THINK ABOUT SIGNIFICANCE

Stage 1

Here are some statements about the Great War. Your teacher may supply them to you on cards, or you can make your own cards. Then take a large piece of paper and draw the six skittles around the edges. Label each one. Put each card next to the skittle it fits with.

> Lots of countries were involved in the war – in fact all the most powerful countries in the world took part.

> More people were killed and wounded than in any previous war.

> The government controlled everyday life more than ever before.

> The war caused immense physical damage and suffering.

> It was the first total war. It affected all of society, both soldiers and civilians.

> Civilians were bombed and shelled for the first time in a war.

> There was fighting in ten different countries.

> Conscription (being forced to fight for your country) was introduced on a grand scale for the first time.

Stage 2

Each of these statements needs evidence to support it. Look back through pages 6–21 to find the evidence you need. The more evidence you can add the better. If you have only a little evidence the skittle may just wobble. If you have lots of evidence it should send the skittle flying. If you have no evidence at all the skittle will be left upright.

Stage 3

The statements in Stage 1 deal mostly with the war itself. Below is another set of statements. These are different. They include some new ideas that you haven't found out about yet. The statements consider some longer term results which you will be studying in later chapters of this book. But some of them will help you now with Significance Alley.

Work with a partner.

1 Rank the statements in order from most significant to least significant. Remember: this is just what *you think*. There are no wrong answers (at this stage).
2 Take your three most significant statements. Which skittles do you think they affect?

> It **changed attitudes** to war. Afterwards, many leaders felt they would do anything to avoid another war like this one.

> **Memorials** to the dead were built in every town and village. Most are still there today.

> It created **new weapons** (such as the tank) and led to **improved technology**, for example better aeroplanes.

> It caused **political chaos** in many European countries. In Germany and Russia there were revolutions. Russia got the first ever communist government.

> It led to the setting up of the first international peace-keeping organisation – **the League of Nations** – to settle disputes between countries peacefully.

> It produced **powerful literature** and **art** such as the war poetry of Wilfred Owen and the paintings of Paul Nash which are now seen as some of the best of the twentieth century.

> It brought changes in the rights and status of **women**.

> Every year, on 11 November, the day the Great War ended, we **commemorate those who died** by wearing poppies, laying wreaths and observing two minutes' silence.

Finally

After you have been through Stages 1–3 note which of the six skittles fell, which wobbled and which stayed upright. Remember that this is only a provisional judgement. It is too early to judge some things – particularly the long term significance.

REVIEW ACTIVITY B

It is hard to get an overview of such a big conflict, but that shouldn't stop us trying. Here is your challenge: from what you have studied on pages 6–21 you have to choose what you think are the three most important facts that *everyone* should know about the Great War.

You can work in groups or individually.

You need to prepare just three PowerPoint slides. Each slide should carry a Great War fact that you think everyone should know. One way of deciding on your facts would be to start with a list of up to ten facts and then cut these down to the top three. You can use a maximum of 25 words on each slide. Prepare a commentary to go with each slide explaining *why* this is an important fact for people to know about the Great War.

FROM WAR TO WAR

Decide how the First World War is linked to the Second World War

◆ *The Treaty of Versailles*

In early 1919 the Allied leaders met in Versailles (near Paris) to agree a peace treaty. Britain, the USA and France were all there. Germany was not invited. This is what the Allies decided:

- ◆ Germany was to **blame** for the war.
- ◆ Germany had to **pay** for all the damage caused by the war. These payments were called REPARATIONS.
- ◆ Germany had to cut down its **army** to just 100,000 men. It had totalled over 2 million in 1914.
- ◆ Germany was forbidden to have an **air force**. Its **navy** was limited to 36 ships and no submarines.

- ◆ Germany lost all its overseas **colonies** which were given to Britain and France to look after.
- ◆ Parts of Germany (including some of its best **industrial areas**) were given to France, Belgium, Poland and other countries.
- ◆ The Treaty also set up a peace-keeping organisation called the **League of Nations**. Germany was not invited to join it.

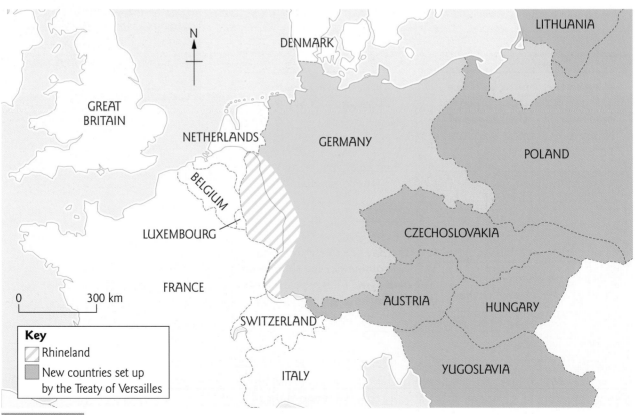

Key
- ▨ Rhineland
- ▦ New countries set up by the Treaty of Versailles

SOURCE 1 A map of Europe after the Treaty of Versailles.

When the terms of the Treaty were announced there was an outcry in Germany. The German people had not expected anything so tough. Germany was proud of its armed forces. To disarm was a deep humiliation, particularly because none of the Allies was disarming.

The Germans did not think they were to blame for the war. Many did not even think they had lost the war. Many Germans had still been expecting victory even in November 1918.

However, German leaders were told they had to sign the Treaty or war would start again. So they did. But to the German people this Treaty was a humiliation that angered them for many years to come.

SOURCE 2 A headline from *Deutsche Zeitung*, a German newspaper.

Vengeance, German Nation! Today a disgraceful treaty is being signed. Do not forget it. The German people will reconquer the place among the nations to which they are entitled. Then will come vengeance for the shame of 1919.

SOURCE 4 A German cartoon published in 1919. The mother is saying to her starving child: 'When we have paid one hundred billion marks, then I can give you something to eat.'

PEACE AND FUTURE CANNON FODDER

The Tiger: "Curious! I seem to hear a child weeping!"

SOURCE 3 A British cartoon from 1920 commenting on the Treaty of Versailles.

ACTIVITY

Working in pairs, look carefully at Sources 3 and 4. These are quite difficult cartoons. See if you can work out what they are saying about the Treaty of Versailles. Discuss them both first. Your teacher can give you some notes to help you.

Then take one cartoon each and write up your summary of what it is saying about the Treaty of Versailles.

◆ How did the Treaty of Versailles help Hitler win support?

In the Great War Adolf Hitler was an ordinary soldier in the German army. He fought hard and won medals for bravery. He was recovering in hospital from a gas attack when the war ended. He was horrified to hear of his country's defeat:

SOURCE 5 He later wrote of this in *Mein Kampf*, 1924.

So it had all been in vain. In vain all those sacrifices. In vain the hours in which, with mortal fear clutching at our hearts, we did our duty.

Then came the Treaty of Versailles. Like many other Germans Hitler felt humiliated by the Treaty. He felt that their leaders had 'stabbed Germany in the back' by signing it. They should have resisted. They should have been stronger and stood firm.

When he had recovered from his war injuries, Hitler joined a tiny political party, the German Workers Party. He soon became its leader. He changed the party's name to the National Socialist German Workers Party, or Nazi Party. He designed its symbol, the swastika (right), and chose its colours. He helped draft the Nazi programme. The opposite page shows some of their ideas. He found audiences ready to listen to him.

Hitler did not believe in democracy. He thought the Nazis should take power by force. In November 1923 he tried to do so, in Munich. This was called the Munich PUTSCH or the Beer-Hall Putsch. It failed. Hitler was sent to prison for nine months. But the putsch and his trial made him famous.

While he was in prison he wrote a book, *Mein Kampf* (My Struggle), which summarised his ideas and aims. When it was published in 1924 it became a best-seller.

SOURCE 6 Hitler wrote in *Mein Kampf* in 1924:

The masses have weak powers of understanding. You must tell them simple things that they want to hear, even if they are lies.

SOURCE 7 Someone who was present at one of the early Nazi meetings describes what it was like.

Hitler knew how to whip up those crowds jammed closely in a dense cloud of cigarette smoke – not by argument, but by his manner: the roaring and repetition. This was a technique he had developed himself and it had a frightening primitive force. He would draw up a list of evils and abuses and, after listing them, in higher and higher crescendo, he screamed: 'And whose fault is it? It's all … the fault … of the Jews!' The beer-mugs would swiftly take up the beat, crashing down on the wooden tables and hundreds of voices, shrill and female or male beer-bellied, repeated the imbecile line for quarter of an hour.

The Nazis then made a big change. They decided that instead of trying to seize power by force they should try to get elected. They started campaigning for elections like normal political parties. Here are some of their election policies:

NAZI POLICIES

Old age pensions should be increased.

The Treaty of Versailles must be abolished.

Germany must take over new territory in Eastern Europe to settle our growing population.

Germany must be allowed to rearm.

The state should take over important industries.

Communism is dangerous and wrong. It must be destroyed.

The state should pay for the education of gifted children.

Germany needs a strong and powerful leader who is able to make it strong again.

Non-Germans should not be allowed to be newspaper editors.

Jews should be removed from all positions of leadership in Germany.

Unemployed people should be recruited as soldiers for the army or employed to build motorways.

We must challenge terror or violence with our own terror or violence.

ACTIVITY

You are a British reporter sent to Germany to research the elections there. Your editor wants to know why the Nazis seem to be popular in Germany.

1 Summarise, using one sentence of your own words, what Hitler was saying on each of these topics:
   a) the Treaty of Versailles
   b) German territory
   c) German people, especially Jews.
2 Take each one of Hitler's policies in turn and show how it would appeal to the German people.

◆ *1936: What would you do?*

In 1933 Germany was in the grip of a terrible depression. Millions of people were unemployed. Businesses were going bankrupt. Hitler's promises to rebuild Germany and make it great again seemed very attractive. The German people voted the Nazis into power. Hitler became Chancellor of Germany.

What happened next was no surprise.

Over the following three years Hitler banned all other political parties, imprisoned his opponents and began persecuting the Jews.

Hitler also began rearming Germany. Remember that under the Treaty of Versailles Germany was supposed to have only a small army, a tiny navy and no air force. Ignoring this entirely, Hitler drafted millions of unemployed into the armed forces. In 1935 he held a massive Freedom to Rearm rally and paraded the new tanks, planes and weapons he was building for all to see.

Then in 1936 Hitler did something quite unexpected. He marched his soldiers into the Rhineland (see map on page 24). This too had been forbidden by the Treaty of Versailles. Most Germans were pleased to see Hitler making Germany strong again. Other countries looked on with alarm. But what could they do? What should they do?

SOURCE 8 German troops going into the Rhineland, 1936.

ACTIVITY

It is 1936. You are at a meeting in Whitehall to discuss the danger to peace presented by Adolf Hitler's invasion of the Rhineland. Senior army, navy and air force commanders are there, as well as government officials. You have three options. Which will you take?

Stage 1: Role play the meeting

1 Work in groups. Each group should appoint a chairperson to lead the discussion. Then each member of the group should decide which option they prefer. The speech bubbles below show some of the arguments that could be used.

> Hitler must be stopped now. He must be taught a lesson. If we let him get away with this who knows what he will do next!

> We need to give a little. Germany was dealt with too harshly under the Treaty of Versailles.

> Hitler is still weak. His rearmament programme is at an early stage. In one or two years' time he will have a powerful, modern, well-equipped army, navy and air force and he'll be much harder to deal with.

Option 1: Send troops to force Hitler to withdraw from the Rhineland

Option 1A: act on our own
Option 1B: act with others

Option 2: Make a deal with Hitler – allow Hitler to keep troops in the Rhineland and get him onto our side

Option 3: Do nothing

There are only two other countries prepared to help get Germany out of the Rhineland: France – but they are in the middle of a depression and weakened by disagreement among their leaders; and the USSR – but that is a communist country and Britain is anti-communist.

The USSR is a worse menace than Hitler because it is communist. A strong Germany is not such a bad idea. Hitler is very anti-communist.

War is terrible – the Great War showed that. We must do anything to prevent going to war.

Events in Europe are nothing to do with us – we aren't affected by them. We should stay out of things like the Americans do.

Britain has a strong navy but only a weak army. Hitler's troops can only be driven out of the Rhineland by a large army.

Germany needs an army to defend itself. Hitler should be allowed to build up his forces to the same level as other nations. That is fair.

2 After the discussion take a vote on what the group will decide to do. (If you choose Option 1 then you will need to go on to consider Options 1A and 1B.)

Stage 2: Write a report

3 You now need to write a brief report outlining the situation.

  a) Explain why Britain seems to be facing the possibility of war again only 18 years after the end of the Great War.

  b) Decide what action the people at the meeting have agreed on. Explain the reasons for their decision. Include at least three points.

  c) Give your own view on the final decision. Do you think it was the right one? Explain why or why not.

You probably found it difficult to role play the meeting on page 29 as if it were 1936 – particularly if you know what really happened. And if you know that three years later Britain found itself at war with Hitler's Germany it is very hard to do indeed. This looking backwards with the benefit of knowing the effect of a decision is called 'hindsight'. Historians sometimes look at events with hindsight, but sometimes they must try to forget it.

DISCUSS

Now that you have studied the period between 1918 and 1939 look back to Significance Alley on pages 22–23. Does anything that happened in this period add to the significance of the Great War or take away from it?

◆ *From 1936 to the outbreak of war*

The British government chose a combination of Options 2 and 3 in 1936. Hitler was allowed to put troops into the Rhineland. Two years later the government again did nothing when he united Germany with Austria (although this was also forbidden under the Treaty of Versailles).

In 1938 Hitler threatened to take over the German-speaking parts of Czechoslovakia. The British Prime Minister, Chamberlain, got Hitler to agree that, if he took over this area, it would be his 'last territorial demand in Europe'. This is known as the Munich Agreement.

Early in 1939 Hitler broke his promise to Chamberlain and took over the rest of Czechoslovakia. Chamberlain could see that Poland would be Hitler's next victim. He made an agreement with Poland that if Hitler invaded, Britain would support it.

In September 1939 German forces invaded Poland. Britain declared war. The Second World War in Europe thus began less than 21 years after the end of the Great War.

WAS THE SECOND WORLD WAR MORE SIGNIFICANT THAN THE FIRST?

The Second World War was more significant than the Great War because ...

it was more of a 'world' war

more people were killed

it created two superpowers who dominated the second half of the twentieth century

it led to the end of the European empires

it crippled Britain

What do you think? Do these things make the Second World War more significant than the Great War?

MEET MAURICE MICKLEWHITE

... and find out how the Second World War changed his life

Maurice Micklewhite was six years old when the Second World War started in September 1939. He lived near the docks in a crowded area of south London called Rotherhithe. With his three-year-old brother, Stanley, he was ordered to go to his school in order to be evacuated.

What was evacuation?

Wars in the past had hardly affected children at all, but twentieth century wars were different. In the First World War 1413 British civilians were killed in air raids. By 1939, aeroplanes were stronger and faster. They carried ten times more bombs than before. Government planners were sure that bombing raids would start as soon as war broke out and that casualties would be horrendous: estimates were made of 50–100 deaths per tonne of bombs dropped. They also feared that gas-bombs would be used.

Well before the war, therefore, plans were made to remove all children from areas thought to be at risk. And on 1 September 1939 the plan was put into effect. One and a half million people – children (and their teachers), pregnant mothers, mothers with young children and disabled people – left home.

The evacuation of 1.5 million people in four days was completed without a single casualty, but the rest of the organisation was poor. Some children were sent to areas, like Sheffield and Plymouth, which were later heavily bombed. No attempt was made to match up children with hosts and evacuation was not always a good experience for those who took part.

SOURCE 1

Maurice Micklewhite

On the day of evacuation my brother and I were up early, eager to start our first great adventure ... The scene at school was pandemonium with harassed teachers trying to get the children lined up in columns of three ... The teachers finally got a grip on the situation and we started off on what turned out to be a two-mile [3.2 km] walk to Waterloo station. I held tightly on to Stanley's hand as we marched, only relinquishing my grip as we turned the corner for one last wave at the band of weeping mothers flapping soggy handkerchiefs. We kept waving until, suddenly, they were gone and Stanley and I were on our own for the first time.

SOURCE 2

Although we were only going about forty miles [64 km] out of London, to Wargrave in Berkshire, the journey took hours but we eventually arrived and were marched to a large village hall where we were greeted with lemonade, sandwiches and large smiling country ladies with red rosy cheeks. We were made to stand in line and the local families came along and inspected us to choose the child they wanted to take care of. Whatever type they were looking for, it was not Stanley and me, and after about an hour he and I were the only two left. Suddenly there was a bustle at the other end of the hall and a wonderful-looking elderly lady came charging towards us. 'Are these the last two?' she said, not unkindly, 'I'll take them.' Then she crouched down and gave us a kiss. Then, for the first time in our lives Stanley and I got into a car. It was bigger than any car I had ever seen; it must have been a Rolls Royce. We were whisked away to a house so big it looked like a castle. There were servants all over the place and we were each shown to lovely little bedrooms. That night I lay in the best bed, in the nicest room, I had ever slept in and thought to myself that this was too good to be true.

It was. The next day Maurice was moved away to the house of people who locked him in the cupboard under the stairs for 24 hours. His mother came and took him home.

Then one year later, when the actual bombing started, his mother moved Maurice and Stanley to rural Norfolk.

SOURCE 3

> We were housed in a disused farmhouse which had been furnished to the standard to which country people expected that slumdwellers from London were accustomed. That is, very primitive. It had oil lamps, wood stoves, tin baths and one outside toilet for ten families.
>
> I had never been so happy in my life. Here was a chance to run free in fresh air, away from the soot-laden fumes of London, and get the sun on my face. There were no chemical fertilisers put on the food we ate, so we were forced to eat organic food for five years. Rationing meant that butter, ice-cream, cream and even milk were rationed so there was no chance of high cholesterol. The government gave all the children free orange juice, cod liver oil, malt, and vitamins, things we would never have had in our diet if there had been no war.

MOTHERS Send them out of London

Give them a chance of greater safety and health

SOURCE 4 Evacuation was not compulsory but posters like this one encouraged mothers to send away their children and to keep them away.

Maurice Micklewhite survived the war. He became an actor when he grew up. He changed his name to Michael Caine and went on to be a world-famous film star. Sources 1, 2, 3 are extracts from his autobiography.

SOURCE 5

ACTIVITY A

You are a reporter on the Rotherhithe local newspaper. Write a rough draft of an article giving an update on the situation one week after evacuation. Include:

◆ a headline
◆ the photo, Source 5 (and write a caption to go with it)
◆ some quotes from eye-witnesses, based on Sources 1–3 in Maurice Micklewhite's account
◆ some mothers' views
◆ an explanation of why evacuation was necessary.

ACTIVITY B

You have read Maurice Micklewhite's story. Do you think his life was changed for better or worse? Why? Think about this and then write down your ideas. Do some research on other evacuees and find out how their lives changed. Your teacher may give you some resource sheets to start you off.

◆ *How did evacuation affect the hosts?*

It wasn't just the 1.5 million evacuees who were changed by evacuation. Many hosts were shocked by the experience. In their sheltered rural communities they had never seen or heard what life was like for some children living in cities.

Within days, people were swapping evacuee 'horror stories' when they met. Soon the newspapers were full of letters and reports about the evacuees' clothes, behaviour, manners, diet and habits. For example:

A   Their clothing was in terrible condition. Some children were sewn into their vests and shirts so they could not change them.

B   Many children had plimsolls as their only footwear.

C   One boy returned to his hosts one day with a live hen under his arm and told his landlady he could 'get plenty more' for her.

D   Many children had lice or fleas. Some had scabies. Most had nits.

E   Except for a few, the children were filthy. Many had not had a bath for months.

F   One boy refused to eat cereal and milk and said, 'I want some bloody beer and chips.'

G   Some children did not get undressed for bed, did not know what pyjamas were and did not sleep in the bed but under it.

H   One six-year-old child peed on the carpet. Her mother, who had travelled with her, told her off, saying 'You dirty thing, messing up the lady's carpet! Go and do it in the corner.'

I   Many evacuees did not know how to use a knife and fork. They were not used to hot meals with green vegetables and asked for slices of bread and margarine which they carried around with them and ate as they played.

DISCUSS

1   Look at the 'reasons' diagram on the next page. Which reasons do you think best explain each of the examples above?

2   Which of the examples do you think you would find it hardest to accept if you were a host? Which would you not be worried about?

Not all evacuees were like this, but for those that were there were different reasons for their behaviour.

Poverty
The 1930s were a bad time for Britain. Millions were unemployed and the 'dole' (unemployment money) was barely enough to live on. Certainly not everyone in the countryside was well off, but many children evacuated from the cities came from homes where there was very little money for clothes, proper beds or decent food.

Bad housing
The housing in Britain's cities was mainly Victorian. Many homes had no bathroom, no running water, and a toilet which was shared with other houses. In Stepney (London) 90 per cent of houses had no bathroom; neither did 40 per cent of houses in Hull and 50 per cent of houses in Glasgow. It was the families in the oldest, poorest parts of cities who were evacuated.

REASONS

Lifestyle
City children lived different lives from country children. They were used to living on the streets, in and out of each others' homes, eating and sleeping when they felt like it. Some children were used to criminal ways and bad language.

Healthcare
These were the days before the National Health Service. A trip to the doctor was too expensive for a poor family. Children would get regular health checks if they went to school but evacuation came at the end of the summer holidays, before school medical inspections had taken place.

ACTIVITY

Do you remember this image?

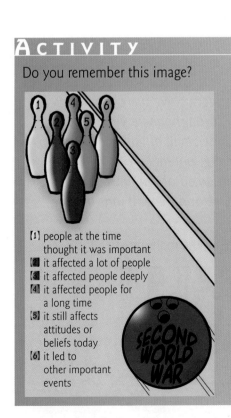

[1] people at the time thought it was important
[2] it affected a lot of people
[3] it affected people deeply
[4] it affected people for a long time
[5] it still affects attitudes or beliefs today
[6] it led to other important events

Over the next 27 pages you will be gathering evidence about the significance of the Second World War. At the end of this section you will see which skittles it knocks down. Was the Second World War a 'strike'?

Start with Maurice Micklewhite. There is plenty in his story to show that the war was significant for him.

1 How would Maurice complete this sentence: 'The Second World War was significant because …'?
2 Which skittle or skittles do Maurice's views relate to?
3 How might one of the hosts of the evacuees finish the sentence in question 1?
4 Which skittle or skittles do their views relate to?

The Blitz is the name given to the bombing of British cities during the Second World War. Liverpool was bombed for four nights in August 1940, then, on 7 September, there was a huge air raid on the London docks. Incendiary bombs caused fires which could be seen for 50 kilometres. On that one night 430 people were killed. The London Blitz went on for 76 nights, then most nights for the next six months.

It would be unfair to try to say which town or city suffered most. London was hit most and longest, with 19,000 tonnes of bombs being dropped. But a big raid on a smaller city could have worse effects. On 14 November 1940 Coventry was bombed: a third of the houses were destroyed and 554 people were killed. In the shipbuilding town of Clydebank, in Scotland, only 7 of the 2000 houses were left inhabitable. By the spring of 1941 most towns and cities in Britain had been bombed, some of them severely.

◆ *Living through a raid*

The warning for an air raid was a siren wailing up and down.

SOURCE 1 Gladys Locke lived in Bristol and was aged 19 when the war broke out. On 23 June 1940 she got married. On 24 June this happened:

We were just going to bed when the siren went. We'd heard it before in practices so we didn't take much notice, but this time I said 'Let's go down the shelter'. The bombs were already dropping and I was shaking and screaming. First came the incendiary bombs. You could tell because the whole garden was lit up, and then came a bomb. The force of the blast took the top of the shelter off. I thought it was the end. All the windows were gone, the doors were off, there was water rushing out because the pipes had been hit, the roof was off and part of the wall. Nearly everything that was breakable in the house was broken. All my wedding presents were gone. Even my wedding cake was full of glass. We had to throw it away.

Later that year, on 24 November, Gladys and her husband were in Bristol city centre for an evening out. They had just begun to walk home when the siren went off:

The walk through the city was, well, I don't think anybody could describe it. There were buildings falling down, there were rescue operations going on with all the people buried in the ruins, there was water gushing through the streets, there were gas mains going. You had to pick your way through where you could get through. But there were fires and the smell of gas and people shouting and screaming, kids crying, parents trying to find their children. And crowds of people huddled about with blankets over them and ambulances running here and there. It was terrible.

SOURCE 2 A street scene in Bristol the morning after an air raid.

Air raid shelters

The most common form of shelter was the Anderson shelter. This was named after Sir John Anderson, Home Secretary at the beginning of the war. Two and a quarter million Anderson shelters were given out free, in kit form. You bolted the curved pieces of corrugated iron to a strong frame, sunk the base one metre into the ground and covered it with half a metre of earth. It could protect up to six people from everything except a direct hit. However, it was damp, too small to sleep in with any comfort and offered no protection against the appalling noise of a raid. You also had to have a garden to put the shelter in. Less than a quarter of families in London had gardens. They relied on shared shelters in public parks. Some people sheltered in underground railway stations.

Plans versus reality

Government planners had expected air raids but they got several things wrong. They had predicted that short, devastating raids would kill millions of people and that millions more would be gassed.

In fact raids were long, sometimes lasting over twelve hours; gas was not used; and deaths were far below expectations. For example, in one raid on London on 15 October 1940, 410 bombers dropped 538 tonnes of high explosive. Pre-war estimates calculated that this level of bombing would kill over 25,000 people. In fact just under 400 were killed.

However, a much bigger problem than expected was the feeding and housing of the homeless, the rescue of and care for the wounded, the comforting of the bereaved, and so on. The sheer number of people affected and the disruption the bombing left in its wake caused the biggest problems. For example, by May 1941, 1.4 million people in London (one in six) were homeless.

SOURCE 3 The 'all-clear' was a long, steady two-minute blast from the air raid siren. When people heard this they left their shelters to see what damage had been done. This mother and child are emerging from their Anderson shelter after a daylight raid on the aircraft works at Filton, Bristol, on 25 September 1940.

◆ *Was the 'Blitz Spirit' all made up by the government?*

SOURCE 4 King George VI and Queen Elizabeth visiting people sheltering in a London Underground station. This photograph was published in newspapers in November 1940.

SOURCE 5 From the *Daily Herald* newspaper, September 1940:

East London paused for a moment yesterday to lick its wounds after what had been planned as a night of terror. But it carried on.

SOURCE 6 Newspapers reported that these signs were put up on bombed buildings, a shop and a pub:

More open than usual

Our windows are gone but our spirits are good. Come in and try them.

ACTIVITY A

Look at Sources 4, 5 and 6. Notice that each was published in a newspaper. What attitude towards the Blitz is each of these newspaper items designed to create?

For many years after the war the popular view was that Britain survived the bombing of its cities because of the 'Blitz Spirit'. So what exactly was this Blitz Spirit?

It was an interpretation of how the Blitz was affecting the British people. It was shown in attitudes to:

◆ The effects of the bombing (see Source 5)
◆ Britain's leaders, like the royal family and Winston Churchill (see Source 4)
◆ Morale (see Source 6).

Why was this 'Blitz Spirit' important? The aim of the bombing was not only to destroy the factories producing the materials of war but also to break the will of the British people to go on fighting. It was therefore vital for the government to keep up people's morale. Britain also desperately needed US war supplies, so it was important to give the impression to the USA, which was not yet in the war, that Britain was keeping up the fight.

The government and newspapers actively tried to promote this Blitz Spirit. News was censored. Sometimes the censor actually wrote the news.

ACTIVITY B

Look at Source 7.
1 What do you think the people in this family are saying and feeling?
2 The actual caption the censor wrote for this photo was: 'ARE THEY DOWN-HEARTED? NO! Blitztown: A Liverpool family, bombed out of their home, rest outside a RECEPTION CENTRE and wonder what they will do next. But there is no sign of sinking spirits, just a good-natured acceptance of fate'.
   What has the censor tried to do by means of the caption he has written?
3 Now look at Source 8. Write your own caption to photograph A or B to make it an example of the 'Blitz Spirit'.

SOURCE 7 A Liverpool family made homeless by an air raid.

SOURCE 8

ACTIVITY C

Was the Blitz Spirit just made up by the government?

Thirty years after the war some historians began to question whether this interpretation told the whole truth. They found evidence that things were not as rosy as all that. Some of the evidence has been included the Evidence File on pages 40–41 in this book.

But does that mean that the 'Blitz Spirit' was **all** made up, all just propaganda?

Look at the Evidence File pages, taking care to read the *attribution* which goes with each source. Think about the sources and decide for yourself how real the Blitz Spirit was. Of course, you only have eight sources here, so your answer will have to start: *'The evidence here suggests...'.*

Blitz Spirit evidence file

SOURCE 9 Mass Observation was an organisation which collected reports on day-to-day life from ordinary people all over the country. The government saw some of these reports but they were not published. The Mass Observation reports were not open to the public until the 1970s. This source is from a report on the big air raid on Coventry in November 1940.

There were more open signs of hysteria observed in one evening than during the whole of the past two months ... Women were seen to cry, to scream, to tremble all over, to faint in the street, to attack a fireman, and so on. There were several cases of suppressed panic as darkness approached. In two cases people were seen fighting to get into cars, which they thought would take them out into the country.

SOURCE 10 A Mass Observation report (see Source 9 for what these reports were), this time on the aftermath of air raids on the East End of London in September 1940.

The press versions of life going on normally in the East End are grotesque. There was no bread, no electricity, no milk, no gas, no telephones. There was every excuse for people to be distressed. There was no understanding in the huge buildings of central London for the tiny crumbled streets of densely massed population.

SOURCE 11 Houses in Stepney, London, destroyed in a raid on 9 September 1940. This picture was suppressed by the censor and not published during the war.

SOURCE 12 Many years after the war, a man who had lived through the Bristol Blitz recalled a visit to the city by Winston Churchill after it had been badly bombed on Good Friday 1941:

They brought Churchill down with some of the top officials of the city. They came to where I lived and they gathered up the school kids from the local schools and gave them flags to wave. There was such hostility from some of the women who had lost friends and relatives that one of the women went and snatched these things away. The police got quite upset. When Churchill actually turned up the women turned on him and started booing and shouting abuse at him.

Not only were they very, very tired, not only were they fed up with the bombing, but they were also very hungry. There was also bad feeling against some of the officials.

SOURCE 13 Years later, Gladys Locke (see Source 1), described how she spent the winter of 1940–41:

We didn't leave Bristol every night, just nights when I had the feeling there might be a raid. My husband just came with me because I was so scared. We would walk miles and sleep in a field, or doze rather, or go to shelter in a village and stay there till the early hours of the morning when there was a bus home. You'd never believe the places we slept in, so cold, so damp. I never cared what it was like, so long as we were out of the raids. You could see the city burning and I would think 'Thank God we're not in it'. After a few weeks of this I was in such a state we took lodgings in a village seven miles [11.2 km] from Bristol.

SOURCE 14 Many years after the war, a man who worked in an aircraft factory in Bristol during the Blitz recalled:

There was very little absenteeism caused by the raids. This was partly because we all felt the raids gave an added importance to our work but much more because we knew if we didn't turn up our mates would be worrying. You would see men staggering at their work from lack of sleep, snatching a ten minute doze in the canteen over their food, and still, when knocking off time came, going off with a cheerful 'See yer in the morning boys!'

SOURCE 15 A famous picture from the Blitz, captioned 'Delivering milk after the raid'.

ORAL **H**ISTORY **R**ESEARCH **T**ASK

Even though the Second World War brought terrible things, many people afterwards looked back on the war years as the best years of their lives. Why should this be? Or is this just another myth?

Find someone you know who lived through the war and ask them to talk about their experiences. How do they remember the war?

SOURCE 16 A leading film-maker wrote to his wife in October 1940:
Some of the damage to London is pretty heart-breaking but what an effect it has had on the people! What warmth – what courage! What determination. People encouraging each other by explaining that if you hear a bomb whistle it means it has missed you. People in the north singing in the public shelters, 'One man went to mow, went to mow a meadow!' WVS girls serving tea to fire-fighters during raids … Everybody secretly delighted with the privilege of holding up Hitler. Certain of beating him. A kind of unselfishness is developing. We have found ourselves on the right side and the right track at last!

A 'WORLD' WAR?

Weigh up the big picture and the small stories, then decide which is more important

◆ The big picture ...

The Second World War was a complicated struggle involving five continents. It is difficult to summarise it all on two pages, but here we show some of the main events.

ACTIVITY

Sources 1–4 show four events in the Second World War.

1 Using the evidence in the timeline and the pictures see if you can work out:
   a) whether these events happened in the European war or the Pacific war
   b) which event from the timeline each source shows
   c) the chronological order of the sources.
2 Which of the pictures show a turning point in the Second World War? Give your reasons. If you are not sure what a turning point is your teacher may give you a sheet to help you.

SOURCE 1

THE WAR IN EUROPE

September 1939– June 1940
German troops conquer much of Western Europe

May 1940
300,000 Allied soldiers are rescued off the beach at Dunkirk, where they have retreated from the advancing German army.

Summer 1940
The Battle of Britain: the RAF fights a fierce air battle to stop Hitler invading Britain. In September Hitler abandons his plan to invade Britain

April 1941
German troops advance into the Mediterranean and North Africa

June 1941– September 1942
German troops invade vast areas of the Soviet Union but they cannot defeat the Red Army. Soviet resistance and severe weather stops their advance

`1940` ———————————— `1941` ———————————— `1942`

December 1941
The Japanese attack the US Pacific Fleet at Pearl Harbor

June 1942
US aeroplanes and aircraft carriers defeat the Japanese navy at the Battle of Midway

THE WAR IN THE PACIFIC

SOURCE 3

SOURCE 2

SOURCE 4

October 1942	**February 1943**	**July 1943**	**June 1944**	**May 1945**
The German army in North Africa is defeated at El Alamein	German forces surrender to the Red Army at Stalingrad. From 1943 the Red Army drives German forces westwards	Allied forces land in Sicily and fight their way north through Italy	D-Day: Allied troops land in northern France and begin to push the German troops out of France and Western Europe	The Russians reach Berlin. Germany surrenders. Hitler commits suicide

| | **1943** | | **1944** | | **1945** | |

By August 1942
Japanese troops conquer many countries and islands around the Pacific, including Hong Kong, Singapore, the Philippines, Malaya, Burma and the East Indies

June 1944
British forces advance into Burma to force out the Japanese

August 1945
The US drops atom bombs on Hiroshima and Nagasaki. Japan surrenders

◆ ... and the small stories

ACTIVITY

1 On a copy of a world map mark the people and the experiences mentioned in the following accounts.
2 Find out if anyone in your class has relatives or friends who fought in the war. Mark these people on the map as well, describing what conditions were like in that part of the war.

The sailors in the Arctic Sea
Britain sent convoys of supply ships to the Soviet port of Murmansk. The ships were often attacked by German aircraft and submarines. The sea was so cold in that area that if a person fell in they died within 90 seconds. The crew of HMS Scylla was there.

The nurse in the desert
The war in North Africa began when the Italians attacked British forces in Egypt. The Italians were driven back, so Hitler sent some of his forces to help them. From 1940 to 1943 the battle swept backwards and forwards across the deserts of North Africa. Here, Nursing Sister Marjorie Bennett describes conditions in the tent hospital she worked at in the North African desert, 1942–43.

The sun was our enemy too. With temperatures of 100[°F] or more for months on end, life became really exhausting. The wards were always full. There were battle casualties of every description, and we were also treating troops for various tropical diseases – sandfly fever, yellow fever, dysentery and also many skin conditions and desert sores. Desert sores were large sunburnt areas, mainly on thighs and arms, that had become septic and ulcerated. Heat exhaustion was another scourge we had to cope with. With little means of reducing body temperature rapidly, due to lack of water and shade, many patients died.

The Sikh in the RAF
Mahinder Singh Pujji was a young Sikh pilot who volunteered for the RAF. He couldn't wait to fly his fighter plane.

I love the Hurricane! I think it was a wonderful aeroplane; I prefer it to the Spitfire. The only snag was its speed. That was a handicap when we were up against German fighters – they were faster than us. But the Hurricane was much more manoeuvrable. I saved my life by making a tight turn. I saw three German fighters in my mirror. I immediately dipped and took such a steep turn. As I finished I could see them miles away. The day I shot down my first aeroplane I just went to my room and lay down. I didn't want to talk to anyone. That could have been my death. That is the reason why the fighter pilot will normally never ever tell you why he has been awarded a medal. I have the DFC [Distinguished Flying Cross] and I hope you don't ask me why either. I know what hell I've gone through but I could never make you realise it.

The German soldier in the USSR

In June 1941 Hitler's armies invaded the USSR, hoping to repeat their successful 1940 conquest of Western Europe. They advanced over 1000 kilometres into the USSR. However, bad roads, huge distances, long supply lines and the country's ferocious winter held them up. Below, Heinrich Haape, a German soldier on the Eastern Front, describes conditions in the winter of 1942–43.

> One night the great freeze-up began and winter was with us, the second grim winter in that accursed country. Like a black cloak the frost folded over the land. A supplies truck came round and brought us greatcoats, gloves and caps with ear-flaps. Despite this, we froze miserably in our funk-holes. In the morning we would be numb with cold, our rifles and guns completely covered with thick hoar-frost. When shells came over the clods of earth which were thrown up were like lumps of granite.
>
> Though apparently healed, last year's frostbite on my heels began to be very painful again. I dared not let myself think how long this cold would be with us, dared not remember that everything will still be frozen up at the end of March. We just sat in our holes and froze, vainly longing to be relieved. But there was no hope whatsoever of relief and that was the worst of all.

The British soldier in the Far East

In 1942, Japanese soldiers captured the British colony of Singapore and then invaded Burma and India, which were key parts of the British Empire. British soldiers were sent out to fight the Japanese. George Dawson from Liverpool was one of them. Here he tells of some of his memories of the war in the Far East.

> Like most of my pals I had never been abroad before. The furthest I'd been was hiking in the Isle of Man. I joined up in 1939 but at first there weren't even enough uniforms and no weapons: we practised using broom handles. The most dangerous thing I'd done before the war was play cricket against fast bowlers. But I was sent to the East. By 1942 I was a gunner, marching through swamps, thigh-high in water, my rifle ready. At any moment I expected to be shot at or attacked by the Japanese, who were experts in jungle fighting. I spent three years fighting in Burma and India. My pals and I were often ill, sometimes frightened, but we stuck together. After the war I never talked about what I had seen or done, not even to my family. I never wanted to go abroad again.

Pujji insisted on wearing his turban while he flew and was allowed to wear a special helmet which came over his turban. But his other religious rules, such as not drinking alcohol, needed some ingenuity to get round:

> As for drinking, I am a good actor. I would shout to the barman, 'Give me a gin and lime, please!' Everyone was too drunk to know exactly what I was drinking. It was water – I had arranged it with the barman. I could do so because I was the Flight Commander, I was the boss. He'd say 'Yes, Sir'. Then the water would come and the Air Marshal or whoever it was would say 'Cheers, Pujji. Good show!'

DISCUSS

1 Which of these five people do you think faced the toughest conditions?
2 Whose story do you think was most significant?
3 Are these 'small stories' more important or less important than the big picture on pages 42 and 43?

Make sure you give reasons for all your answers.

Join the debate: was Truman right to do it?

◆ Background: how did the war in the Pacific begin?

Early morning, Sunday 7 December 1941. Pearl Harbor, in Hawaii, was peaceful. US warships – most of the Pacific fleet – were lying in neat rows in the harbour. Sailors were dozing on the decks. A band was practising. Lines of aeroplanes rested on the concrete runways. No one was at the anti-aircraft guns – after all, the USA was not at war. Some of the guns had no ammunition with them 'because it got dusty'.

Meanwhile, 300 kilometres to the north, 183 Japanese fighter-bombers were taking off from aircraft-carriers. They headed for Pearl Harbor. Within minutes they arrived at their target and the bombing began. Two hours later a second wave of Japanese bombers arrived. The results of the bombing can be seen in Source 1.

By the time the Japanese bombers left, 3 battleships had been sunk, 3 more warships were crippled, 188 aircraft had been destroyed, 159 more were damaged and 2403 people had been killed. Why had the Japanese done this? Why had they attacked the strongest nation in the world, provoking the USA into war? Had their leaders gone mad?

No, the Japanese leaders had not gone mad. They knew the industrial and military strength of the USA. They knew this attack was a big gamble. But they also believed that if their country were to survive as a proud, independent nation they would have to fight the USA sometime. To General Tojo, Chief Minister of Japan, December 1941 seemed the ideal moment to strike.

SOURCE 1 US battleships burning at Pearl Harbor.

SOURCE 2 Extent of Japanese conquests by 1942.

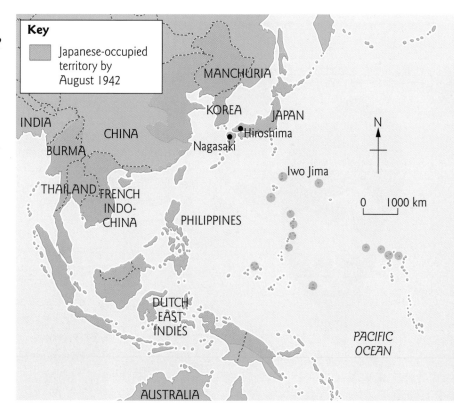

Key

Japanese-occupied territory by August 1942

MANCHURIA

KOREA

JAPAN

INDIA

CHINA

Hiroshima

BURMA

Nagasaki

N

THAILAND FRENCH INDO-CHINA

PHILIPPINES

Iwo Jima

0   1000 km

DUTCH EAST INDIES

PACIFIC OCEAN

AUSTRALIA

1 We have a large and growing population crammed onto the four main islands which make up Japan.

2 Much of Japan is rocky and infertile. We need more land!

3 We don't have good supplies of essential raw materials. We have no oil, no rubber.

4 Other nations have built up empires. The French, the British, the Dutch and the USA all have colonies around the Pacific. Why shouldn't we have an empire, too?

5 War is a great and honourable tradition for us. Our army manual states: 'Bear in mind that to be captured is a disgrace to the Army and the Emperor. Also your parents and family will never be able to hold up their heads again. Always save the last bullet for yourself.'

General Tojo's thoughts

6 The 1930s Depression made our economic problems much worse.

7 In 1931 we successfully invaded and seized Manchuria. Some nations protested, but no one stopped us!

8 In 1936 we made an alliance with Hitler's Germany.

9 Since 1937 we have been at war with China. We have captured many towns and cities in that huge and disorganised country.

12 In July 1941 we successfully seized French Indo-China. No one could stop us. Only the USA stands in the way of our building up a huge empire.

11 In 1940 France and the Netherlands were defeated by our allies, Germany. They are unable to protect their colonies. Britain is fighting for her life and cannot protect hers.

10 In 1940 we military leaders took over the government of our country, putting an end to democracy, and enabling us to plan for war in secret.

13 The USA has stopped selling oil to us. We used to get 80 per cent of our oil from the USA. We need oil to continue our war with China and to build our empire. Are we going to bow down to these white men and look foolish?

14 If we strike now, while everyone else has their eyes fixed on the war in Europe, we could cripple the US Pacific Fleet in a surprise attack. If they don't have ships they can't fight a war with us in the Pacific. If this wins us a two-year start, we shall then be too strong for even the USA to dislodge us!

ACTIVITY

Why did Tojo bomb Pearl Harbor?

Look at the thoughts of General Tojo above. All help to explain Tojo's decision. You have to decide how to *group* the thoughts. How can you group them to make a convincing explanation? There are a number of possible patterns:

◆ you could put together those factors that were under Japanese control and those that were not
◆ you could group together long-term and short-term factors
◆ you could decide on less important and more important factors
◆ you could group the thoughts by theme.

Choose whichever structure you feel will help you write the best answer to the above question. Your teacher may then give you a sheet to help you get started.

◆ *How did the atomic bomb end the war in the Pacific?*

General Tojo's gamble failed. When his bombers arrived above Pearl Harbor they found that the most important ships of all, the aircraft carriers, were not there – they were out at sea.

The USA recovered from its losses at Pearl Harbor much more quickly than Tojo hoped. Only six months later, in June 1942, the US fleet defeated the Japanese fleet at the Battle of Midway.

From then on the USA and its allies (including Britain) gradually drove back the Japanese forces towards Japan.

By the summer of 1945, the Japanese were clearly defeated. Huge, almost unopposed, air raids were launched on Japanese cities – 84,000 people died in a raid on Tokyo on 9 March 1945. But still surrender seemed to be unthinkable to Japanese leaders.

The obvious next move was to invade Japan, but US commanders were concerned about the potential cost of lives. The Japanese defenders of the island of Iwo Jima, near Japan, had fought almost to the last man: 22,400 out of the GARRISON of 23,000 had died. They had taken 23,000 US soldiers with them. What would it be like if US troops tried to land on the sacred soil of Japan itself? Some feared it could take the Americans years and cost hundreds of thousands of lives.

There was another option: since 1941, Allied scientists, many of them refugees from Nazi Europe, had been working in the USA on the 'Manhattan Project'. Their task was to develop a bomb which used ATOMIC FISSION to release huge amounts of energy in a single reaction. In July 1945 they exploded a test bomb in the New Mexico desert. As the ball of fire rose 12,000 metres above the site, the watching scientists measured the explosion as approximately equivalent to 20,000 tonnes of TNT (a high explosive). They had just enough material for two more bombs.

The US President, Harry S. Truman, ordered one of these bombs to be used on the Japanese city of Hiroshima. On 6 August 1945 a single plane, the *Enola Gay*, dropped the bomb, timed to explode 570 metres above the ground. Some 80,000 people were killed. Other results of the bombing are presented on these pages.

Three days later a second bomb was dropped, on the city of Nagasaki.

The Japanese asked for peace. This was agreed just over three weeks later, on 2 September 1945.

SOURCE 3 Hiroshima after the bomb. This devastation was caused by just one bomb.

SOURCE 4 The Reverend Kiyoshi Tanimoto, a Methodist minister, gave this account of what happened to him in Hiroshima on 6 August 1945. He was speaking to US journalist John Hersey a year after the bombing. The account is written in Hersey's words.

A tremendous flash of light cut across the sky. He had time to react as he was about two miles [3.2 km] from the centre of the explosion and threw himself between two big rocks in the garden. He felt a sudden pressure and then splinters and pieces of board and tile fell on him. When he dared he raised his head and saw that the house had collapsed. He thought a bomb had fallen directly on it. Under a huge dust cloud, the day grew darker and darker...

Tanimoto's wife and baby were staying with friends on the other side of the city. He decided he had to see if they were all right and began to run into the city:

He was the only person making his way into the city. He met hundreds who were fleeing and every one seemed to be hurt in some way. The eyebrows of some were burnt off and skin hung from their faces and hands. Others, because of the pain, held up their arms as if carrying something. Some were vomiting as they walked. Many were naked or in shreds of clothing. On some, the burns had made patterns – of undershirt straps and, on the skin of some women, the shapes of the flowers on their kimonos (since white repelled the heat from the bomb and dark colours absorbed it and conducted it to the skin).

After crossing the bridges, he saw, as he approached the centre, that all the houses had been crushed and many were on fire. The trees were bare and their trunks charred. Under many houses people screamed for help, but no one came.

By an incredible stroke of luck he met his wife and baby and saw them safely back to the suburbs before returning to the city to see if he could help. He found many of the dead and seriously injured lying in Asano Park:

He was angry at the doctors and decided to bring one to Asano Park, by the scruff of the neck if necessary. He crossed the river and found an army medical unit. He could see they were hopelessly over-burdened, with thousands of patients sprawled among the corpses ... Nevertheless he went up to one of the army doctors. 'Why have you not come to Asano Park? You are badly needed there.'

'The first duty', the doctor said, 'is to take care of the slightly wounded.'

'Why, when there are many who are heavily wounded?'

The doctor moved to another patient. 'In an emergency like this,' he said, 'the first task is to help as many as possible. There is no hope for the heavily wounded. They will die. We can't bother with them.'

ACTIVITY

On the next two pages you are going to prepare for a debate: **Was Truman right to drop the bomb?** To help you prepare, work in pairs to list as many reasons as you can think of under each of these headings:

◆ Yes – he was right
◆ No – he was wrong.

SOURCE 5 A victim of the Hiroshima bomb, showing the results of burns.

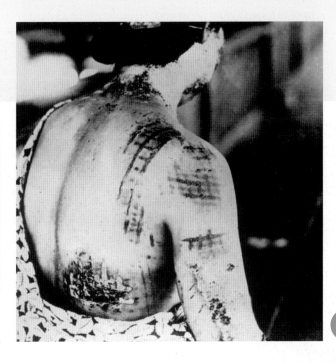

49

THE GREAT DEBATE: WAS TRUMAN RIGHT TO DROP THE BOMB?

ACTIVITY

Although Truman was sure he had done the right thing, he faced mounting criticism. The debate over whether he made the right decision continues to this day. Now it's time to have your say.

The big question for debate breaks down into the smaller questions listed in the table below. Make your own copy of this table. Then use the text and sources on pages 46–51 to fill in evidence supporting either side of the debate. When you have done this your teacher can give you a sheet to help you write a speech for the debate.

Questions	Yes	No
1 Were the **casualties** justified?		
2 Was it necessary to drop the bomb? Were there **alternatives**?		
3 Were Truman's **motives** acceptable?		

3

Saburo Hayashi, secretary to the Japanese War Minister in 1945, said in an interview in 1963:

We were prepared to stage the decisive battle on the Japanese mainland. We thought we could defeat the Americans on their first landing attempt, but if they launched a second or third attack, first of all our food supplies would run out. We didn't have a sufficient amount of weapons, nor could we have made more. Therefore, if the Americans had chosen to come without haste, the Japanese forces would have eventually put their hands up without the Americans resorting to atomic bombs.

4

The Campaign for Nuclear Disarmament is strongly opposed to all nuclear weapons. In 1985 it suggested that Truman had other motives for using his atomic bombs:

General Groves, the engineer director of the Manhattan Project, was desperate to see the fruits of his labours before the war ended. The bomb had been developed at a cost of $2 billion. It would have been difficult to justify not using it after such a vast financial investment. Two types of bomb had been developed. Nagasaki was simply an experiment to try out the second type.

1

Most people in Britain at the time supported Truman. A poll carried out in 1945 gave Truman 72 per cent support. In the USA this figure was even higher. Truman himself never had any doubts. Speaking in 1958 he said: 'Hell no, I made the decision, like', and he snapped his fingers, 'like that!' He wanted to end the war quickly and save American lives – and he succeeded.

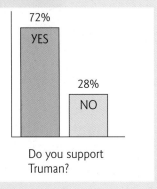

Do you support Truman?

2

The atom bomb was more destructive than any before in history.

Ninety-five per cent of the people within 800 metres of the bomb died at once and so did many more who were further away. Most were simply evaporated by the extreme heat, which scientists later calculated at 6000°C. Others were killed by burning or collapsing buildings.

As time went by, new symptoms and causes of death appeared. People's hair fell out, their kidneys failed, vomiting and diarrhoea led to a slow death. Cancers, particularly leukaemia, increased. Babies were born with deformities, even those conceived after the bomb was dropped. The Japanese called those who were affected by the bombs on Hiroshima or Nagasaki *hibakushas* (people who have been bombed). These people found it hard to find jobs or marriage partners.

In the ten years after 1945, 60,000 more people died, the victims of RADIATION sickness. However, in 1945 US scientists did not know what the long-term effects of the bomb would be.

5
This cartoon was published in the *Evening Standard* in 1960. Note the text in the top left of the cartoon.

9
President Truman could only work with the information he had available. He did not know how strong or weak the Japanese were.

10
There will always be casualties in war – but Japanese casualties were not excessive. More people were killed by Allied bombing in Germany than by the bombing of Hiroshima and Nagasaki.

6
Was Truman more interested in scaring the USSR than in ending the war with Japan? Many years after the war a reporter remembered an 'off-the-record' conversation he had had with James Byrnes, a senior adviser to President Truman, in Europe in 1945. Byrnes had said:

Can I tell you what really worries me? The USSR's spreading influence. The countries of Eastern Europe are all living under the Soviet shadow. It will be impossible to persuade the USSR to remove her troops unless she is impressed by American military might. Now our possessing and demonstrating the bomb will make the USSR more manageable.

8
The Japanese did not believe in surrender. They would fight to the death as they did at Iwo Jima (see page 48). Even after the second bomb on Nagasaki there was still a group of Japanese generals who tried to seize power from the Emperor because he was ready to surrender to the Allies. They wanted to continue the war whatever the cost.

This photo shows a soldier who has chosen to kill himself rather than surrender.

11
The mushroom cloud over Hiroshima after the bomb exploded. The blast raised dust and debris 20 kilometres into the air and spread radioactive material over hundreds of kilometres.

7
Instead of bombing Japan a demonstration could have been arranged. Some of the Manhattan Project scientists suggested to Truman in 1945:
A demonstration of the bomb might best be made on the desert or on a barren island. Japan could then be asked to surrender.

12
It actually saved lives. Millions more soldiers and civilians might have died in an invasion.

The Holocaust is the name that historians give to the systematic killing by the Nazis of at least 6 million Jews (including 1 million children) and 4 million other civilians during the Second World War.

We all know people can be cruel to one another, but such barbaric treatment of one group of human beings by another seems almost unbelievable. So your first task in this enquiry is to investigate how and why this could have happened.

ACTIVITY

Explaining the Holocaust is not simple. There was not just one cause. Many different causes worked together to make it happen.

Make a copy of this basic timeline. Your task over the next six pages is to add notes in the boxes to explain what happened at each stage and how this helped cause the Holocaust.

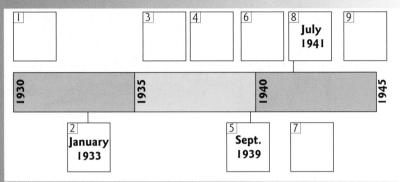

| 1 | | 3 | 4 | 6 | 8 July 1941 | 9 |

1930 — 1935 — 1940 — 1945

| 2 January 1933 | | 5 Sept. 1939 | 7 |

Use the information on these two pages to add notes to your timeline. You should be able to fill in boxes 1–4.

BOX 1

ANTI-SEMITISM IN EUROPE

Anti-Semitism means hatred of Jews. For centuries Jews had suffered persecution. They had been driven out of England in the Middle Ages, and they had been attacked in other countries too. In Russia there had been pogroms (attacks) which had caused many Jews to leave Russia to live in safer countries such as Germany. By the 1920s there were half a million Jews living in Germany. They were happy there. They thought of themselves as Germans. Many had fought for Germany in the First World War.

BOX 2

THE RISE OF HITLER

Hitler was a racist. He believed that black people, Gypsies and other non-whites were inferior to white people. He believed that ARYANS were the master race and they had a right to rule over other races. Hitler was violently anti-Jewish (anti-Semitic).

While the Nazis were still a weak party, Hitler's extremist views did not harm the Jews. But in January 1933 Hitler became Chancellor of Germany (see page 28). Now all the powers of a twentieth-century state were at his disposal. He could make whatever laws he wanted. The Jews and all other minority groups were now at his mercy.

SOURCE 1 Hitler, in the crowd at a rally, in the early 1920s.

BOX 3

THE DISCRIMINATION BEGINS

■ **In April 1933** Hitler ordered a boycott of shops owned by Jews.

■ **Also in April 1933** the Nazis set up their first prison camp, at Dachau. This was run by Hitler's personal guard, the SS. Political opponents of the Nazis were the main group to be imprisoned in this camp but many Jews were arrested too. Jewish prisoners were treated cruelly.

■ **In 1935** Hitler passed the Nuremberg Laws, including:

SOURCE 2 Nazi soldiers carry placards saying 'Germans! Defend yourselves! Do not buy from Jews!' in Berlin in 1933.

✗ Marriage between Jews and citizens of Germany is forbidden.
✗ Sexual relations between Jews and citizens of Germany are forbidden.
✗ Jews may not employ female citizens under 45 years old.
✗ No Jew can be a German citizen.

BOX 4

KRISTALLNACHT

In 1938 some Jews were expelled from Germany and dumped over the border in Poland, to live in squalor in a stable for weeks. The 17-year-old son of one of them was so furious that he assassinated a German diplomat. There was a howl of outrage from the Nazis. They planned a tremendous attack on Jews, their property and their synagogues. It has come to be called *Kristallnacht* (Broken glass night) from the amount of windows smashed. But over 1000 Jews were killed; 1118 synagogues were destroyed or damaged; and the Jews of Germany had to pay a 'fine' of 1 billion marks to repair the damage.

 EYEWITNESS

Walter was born in 1920 in Wiesbaden. He was a Jew. His ancestors had lived in Germany since the Middle Ages. His father was a well-known doctor, much respected in the community by Jews and non-Jews alike. In 1989 Walter was asked how his parents had reacted to the growing discrimination.

SOURCE 3

I can't say what my parents specifically said, but the general idea that German Jews had then was: We have lived in this country for hundreds of years. This guy Hitler, he's from Austria, he's not even German. He's talking big – he's got to say all these things to attract attention – but he isn't going to do all the bad things that he says. There's a German proverb: 'soup is not eaten as hot as it is cooked'. In the next election we're going to vote him out of office again.

This was all gradual, just a little bit at a time. You see, if Kristallnacht had happened in '33 the Jews would have been out of there. All of them. But it was gradual and you kind of get used to it.

BOX 5

THE WAR BEGINS

In September 1939 the Second World War began. This was a turning point. German forces invaded Poland and then the western USSR. At this time there were only half a million Jews living in Germany. But Poland and the USSR were the heartlands of Europe's Jewish population; 5 million Jews lived there. They had their own language, Yiddish. They had their own newspapers, theatres, books and cinemas. There was a thriving Jewish culture.

SOURCE 4 German troops about to set off for Poland in September 1939. The words scrawled on the carriage read: 'We're off to Poland to thrash the Jews.'

BOX 6

THE GHETTOS

On 20 September 1939, all Jews in Nazi-occupied territory were ordered to move into special parts of certain cities, called ghettos. They were cut off from the rest of the city by walls, barbed wire and armed guards. These were desperately over-crowded places. The Warsaw ghetto measured just 4.1 square kilometres and held half a million people. There were ten to fourteen people to a room. If someone tried to leave the ghetto they could be shot.

The Nazis made a point of humiliating strict Jews, particularly rabbis. One rabbi asked to be allowed to continue to wear his beard (it is a religious rule of strict Jews not to shave). The Nazi police chief said he could buy this right for a hundred lashes of the whip. After ten strokes the old man fainted and spent two weeks in hospital.

Food supplies to the ghettos were strictly controlled. The ration was about 1000 calories per day, sometimes much less; a working adult needs at least 2000 calories a day to keep alive. People fought over food. Children became smugglers and beggars.

Thousands of Jews escaped from the ghettos to join resistance groups which fought the Germans and hid Jews. There were also revolts in many ghettos. In the Warsaw ghetto uprising of 1943, Jews with only a few weapons between them held off the Nazi army for nearly a month. But in the end they were beaten. In revenge, the Nazis killed thousands.

SOURCE 5 People selling rags in a Warsaw ghetto, 1941.

BOX 7

THE *EINSATZGRÜPPEN*

Special squads of soldiers, called *Einsatzgrüppen*, were sent into Eastern Europe to round up Jews and shoot them. It is estimated that 2 million Jews were killed in this way.

SOURCE 6 Einsatzgrüppen shooting Jews.

ACTIVITY

Use the information on these two pages to add notes to your timeline (see page 52). You should be able to fill in boxes 5–7.

DISCUSS

Study Sources 7 and 8.
Who is most to blame for these events?

◆ The ordinary German soldiers who fired the guns
◆ The officers who gave the orders
◆ The army generals
◆ Hitler.

 # EYEWITNESSES

SOURCE 7 The testimony of SS officer August Hafner:

I went to the woods alone. The army had already dug a grave. The children were brought along in a tractor. The children were taken down. They were lined up along the top of the grave and shot so that they fell into it. The wailing was indescribable. I shall never forget the scene throughout my life. I find it very hard to bear.

I particularly remember a small fair-haired girl who took me by the hand. She too was shot.

SOURCE 8 Helen L. was a Jewish girl who lived in Eastern Europe with her large, happy family – she had nine brothers and sisters. Helen was 12 when the *Einsatzgrüppen* came.

I had wonderful parents, truly wonderful people. My father was exceptional. I loved my mother very much. I absolutely idolised my Dad. To me he was God. If he stood next to me I knew nothing could possibly go wrong.

My father and brothers were taken to a place called Kamenets Podolsk. They were taken to a mass grave. The soldiers, of course, made them dig the grave. Then they ran machine guns where my Dad and my four brothers were. My father and three brothers got killed. My fourth brother Max fainted as the machine gun ran. He fell into that grave. During the night, when he came to, he pulled himself out of that grave from under all the bodies. Moving only at night in the fields of high wheat, he crossed the border into Russia. He spent the remainder of the war there.

BOX 8

THE FINAL SOLUTION

SOURCE 9 In July 1941 Hitler's close colleague Göring gave orders to Himmler and Heydrich, other top Nazis:

I hereby charge you with making all necessary preparations for bringing about the final solution of the Jewish question within the German sphere of influence in Europe.

DISCUSS

Look at Source 9. The language – the actual words used – is important.

1 How does Göring refer to the Jews?
2 What do you think he means by 'the final solution'?
3 Why do you think he hasn't said what he means more clearly?

ACTIVITY A

Use the information on these two pages to add notes to your timeline (see page 52). You should now be able to fill in boxes 8 and 9.

BOX 9

THE DEATH CAMPS

Even shooting innocent, defenceless people in cold blood was not enough for the Nazi Party. In January 1942 Nazi leaders met at a conference at Wannsee to decide how to put to death all Jews living under Nazi rule. Gas chambers were built at Auschwitz, in Poland, capable of killing 2000 people at once. Auschwitz was chosen because of its good railway links with the rest of Europe. Later, other death camps were built at Chelmno, Belzec, Maidenek, Sobibor and Treblinka. (Note that none of these places is in Germany itself.)

A highly-efficient system of killing was set up. From all the Nazi-occupied areas of Europe, from Norway to Greece, the Netherlands to Romania, Jews (plus Gypsies, homosexuals, Jehovah's Witnesses – anyone the Nazis wanted to get rid of) were methodically rounded up, listed, put into cattle-trucks with little food, water or sanitation, and sent to one of the camps. Some of the journeys from the more remote parts of Europe took several days. Even before reaching the camps, 320,000 people died on the trains.

SOURCE 10 Dutch Jewish women on the train to Auschwitz.

SOURCE 11 The prisoners were lined up on the 'ramp', a raised platform. They walked past the SS commander, who determined each person's fate: to one side, all those who he thought were fit enough to work went to crowded barracks; to the other, death. About 80 per cent of the people on each train went straight to the gas chamber.

👁 EYEWITNESSES

SOURCE 12 Helen L. (see Source 8 on page 55) was sent to Auschwitz. She was one of the few chosen for work.

We were asked to strip, totally, and waited, lined up, many of us. You have to understand that we were so much more modest, that even in front of your own Dad I don't think you would ever go with less than a full slip. And there we are standing totally in the nude and all the people that shaved our heads, everywhere were men. We stood naked for hours and hours, and after that we went through a place which was like a shower, but it wasn't water, it was like a disinfectant. And then we were given those striped dresses, with no underwear. The shoes you were wearing you left.

We still were not aware of the fact that we were separated and I was never to see my mother again. When I was in Auschwitz about two or three days, I asked a Nazi lady, I said, 'Where's my mother?' And she being all heart, pointed to the chimney. She said, 'You see that smoke coming out? That's probably her.' And that's, that was really the first time that it hit. This is where we are. This is what is happening.'

Helen L. was transferred from Auschwitz to another camp. She survived there until the war was almost over, when all the prisoners were taken out of the camps and marched away from the advancing enemy. She escaped from the march and ended the war in a refugee camp. She now lives in the USA.

DISCUSS

1 Asked when he thought the Holocaust began, historian Martin Gilbert replied: 'When the first Jew was treated differently from other Germans.' Do you agree? Use the evidence on your timeline to support your answer.

2 Looking at your completed timeline, how did each of the following contribute to the Holocaust?
   a) Anti-Semitism in Europe
   b) Hitler's racism
   c) Other Nazi leaders
   d) Nazi soldiers who joined the *Einsatzgrüppen* or who worked in the camps.

ACTIVITY B

In 2001 the British government introduced Holocaust Memorial Day. This is commemorated on 27 January each year. Write a short paragraph to go on your school website explaining why the Holocaust is such a significant event that it should be remembered in this way.

SOURCE 13 Jewish children in the Polish town of Nowogrodek in 1936. From left to right: Seindl Sucharski, 12, killed; Srolik Sucharski, 10, killed; Leizer Kagan, 9, killed; Leizer Senderowski, 21, escaped to Russia; Jack Kagan, 7, joined the partisans and survived; Nachama Kagan, 10, killed; Dov Kagan, 12, joined the partisans and survived.

Trace the consequences of the Second World War

ACTIVITY

Each of these six pictures shows an event that is linked to the Second World War. At the bottom of the page are six labels explaining the links.

1 Which of the labels in the boxes do you think explains which event?
2 Which event do you think is the most important consequence of the Second World War? Give your reasons.

1948 Indians celebrate independence from Britain

SECOND

1960 Soviet and US tanks face each other over the Berlin Wall

1957 The Treaty of Rome: the founding of the European Economic Community

1 The war had weakened and bankrupted the European powers. They could not spend money holding on to their colonies in Africa and Asia.

2 After the devastation of two world wars the people and leaders of countries in western Europe believed that the way forward for Europe was to cooperate with each other, not fight each other.

3 People realised that the world needed a stronger organisation than the League of Nations to settle disputes between countries if more awful wars were to be prevented.

1992 A UN peace-keeping mission in the former Yugoslavia

1948 The foundation of Israel

WORLD WAR

1945 Hiroshima: after the bomb

4 The suffering of the Jewish people in the Holocaust made many other countries sympathetic to the idea of establishing the state of Israel as a Jewish homeland in Palestine.

5 Two countries emerged more powerful than the rest from the Second World War: the USSR and the USA. They had fought together as allies against Hitler but once Hitler was beaten they did not agree about anything. They were soon in conflict with each other.

6 The huge destructive power of nuclear weapons made the world feel much less safe.

WHY DID WILLIAM BEVERIDGE TAKE ON THE FIVE GIANTS?

Write a back cover blurb for the Beveridge Report

Before the Second World War poverty was a big problem in Britain. Millions were unemployed. Many people in cities lived in old and run-down slum housing. Education was compulsory but many schools had poor facilities. Medical care cost money so only the rich could afford the best treatment. Governments seemed unable or unwilling to do anything. The war changed that.

◆ Reason 1: Increased awareness

The war opened the eyes of people in Britain to each other. It wasn't that those who lived in better-off areas before the war didn't care about the people who lived in the slums: their lives just didn't meet. The war had broken that ignorance wide open. People who would never have talked to each other in peacetime met in the shelters, in the army, in the queues, in the factories, on the trains. The rich and powerful could see the great poverty all around them. As we have seen in this chapter:

- the bombing in the Blitz brought terrible hardship, and most affected those living in crowded slum housing
- bombing destroyed thousands of houses. Hundreds of thousands were homeless and would need new houses after the war
- to help control food supplies the government had introduced rationing. They could now see how poor the diet of ordinary people was
- everyone had to manage on the same government rations

- evacuation forced well-off people to take in children from some of the most deprived areas. The hosts were shocked by the habits, the diet, the clothes and the hygiene of evacuee children
- caring for victims of the Blitz highlighted how inadequate health care provision was for poor people in many cities and towns.

◆ Reason 2: Something to look forward to

Everyone in Britain was asked to make personal sacrifices for the country's war effort. Government wartime propaganda played up patriotic feelings. But there had to be more than just patriotism: the government had to offer hope for the future. At the height of the war, when it was not even clear that Britain would survive, let alone win, plans were made for a better Britain. Sir William Beveridge was put in charge of suggesting far-reaching changes to the system of welfare in Britain.

your **BRITAIN** · fight for it now

ISSUED BY A.B.C.A.

SOURCE 1 A government poster.

◆ *The Beveridge Report, 1942*

Beveridge's report in 1942 was very radical. It said there were 'Five Giants' that prevented people from leading decent lives (see below) and set out to defeat them all.

The Beveridge Report was pretty boring to read, yet it sold 635,000 copies. People talked about it everywhere.

Even before the end of the war the government put some recommendations into action. The Town and Country Planning Act of 1943 protected the countryside by creating 'green belts' of land. The Education Act of 1944 overhauled the way schools were organised.

Most people believed Labour would put Beveridge's proposals into action; Labour won the 1945 election with a big majority. Over the next six years changes were introduced which still form the basis of Britain's welfare system today.

◆ National Insurance, 1946. Every working person pays money to the government out of their wages; in return, the state helps out with cash when they can't earn, owing to sickness, old age, pregnancy or unemployment.

◆ National Assistance, 1948. This was to help anyone still in financial difficulties who needed further help. It still exists under different names today.

◆ National Health Service, 1948. This gave free health care for everyone, including doctor's visits, dentistry, medicines and hospital care. Today not all of these are completely free, but the basic idea remains the same: no one should be stopped from seeking treatment for fear of not being able to afford it.

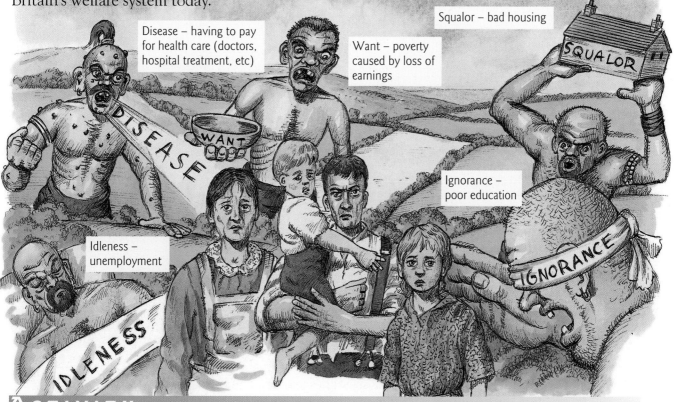

Disease – having to pay for health care (doctors, hospital treatment, etc)

Want – poverty caused by loss of earnings

Squalor – bad housing

Ignorance – poor education

Idleness – unemployment

ACTIVITY

You have been asked to write a simple 100-word blurb for the back cover of the Beveridge Report, explaining the reasons for the report and why everyone should read it. You might also like to suggest a new title and a cover picture, and write some reviews. Make sure it is clear to your readers why this book is significant.

REVIEW ACTIVITY A

Was the Second World War more significant than the First?

Do you remember Significance Alley? You first met it on page 4. Each of the skittles represents a criterion for significance. Your task is to use what you have found out about the Second World War to see which skittles it knocks down. To show that the war knocks down a skittle you will need to find evidence that it meets this criterion.

THINK ABOUT SIGNIFICANCE

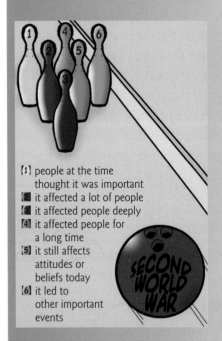

[1] people at the time thought it was important
[2] it affected a lot of people
[3] it affected people deeply
[4] it affected people for a long time
[5] it still affects attitudes or beliefs today
[6] it led to other important events

SECOND WORLD WAR

For the same task about the Great War we helped you by providing statements for you to sort. This time you are on your own. Working with a partner or in a group, write down all the evidence you can think of that would hit any of the skittles. You don't need to sort your evidence yet, just brainstorm your ideas. Write each one on a separate piece of paper or card.

Now take a large piece of paper. Draw the six skittles on it and label them. Then move each of your cards next to the skittle it fits with. The more evidence you can add the better. If you have only a little evidence maybe the skittle will just wobble. If you have lots of evidence it should send the skittle flying. If you have no evidence at all the skittle will be untouched.

When you have finished, note which of the six skittles fell, which wobbled and which stayed upright. Was this more of a strike or less of a strike than the Great War?

REVIEW ACTIVITY B

Your challenge is to prepare a PowerPoint presentation which uses three slides. Each slide should carry a Second World War fact that you think everyone should know. One way of working would be to start with a list of up to ten facts and then cut these down to the three most important. Work in groups if you prefer. You can use a maximum of 25 words on each slide. Prepare a commentary to go with each slide explaining *why* this is an important fact for people to know about the Second World War.

REVIEW ACTIVITY C

The Second World War is often referred to as a 'People's War'. What could this mean?

◆ That ordinary people suffered more than fighting men.
◆ That ordinary people had the greatest impact on the war effort.
◆ That the war was fought in order to change the lives of ordinary people.

1 What evidence can you find in this section to support each of these meanings?
2 Use this evidence to explain whether you think the Second World War *was* a 'People's War'.
3 Do you think it was more of a 'People's War' than the First World War?

THE COLD WAR

The Cold War is the name given to the rivalry between the CAPITALIST USA and the communist USSR between 1945 and 1990.

The Cold War was different from the other wars because...

it lasted longer – forty-five years

the two sides hardly ever fought each other directly

it killed millions of people

it scared everyone

it could have destroyed the world

... and I'm not sure it's really over yet.

Is the Cold War still significant?

ACTIVITY

The man in Source 1 is Conrad Schumann. What do you think he is doing?

1 Use the statements on page 65 to unravel the mystery. You could begin by dividing the statements into groups about:

◆ Conrad or his family
◆ Berlin
◆ the Berlin Wall
◆ capitalism and communism.

2 When you have worked out what happened, use the statements to write a headline and a two-paragraph account for the front page of a newspaper. Tell your readers why Conrad jumped.

SOURCE 1

At school Conrad's teacher said he was very good at English. Conrad was also a keen athlete and especially good at the long jump.

Standards of living in East Berlin were lower than in West Berlin. In the 1950s lots of East Germans escaped to West Germany in search of a better life.

On 13 August 1961 trucks arrived with lots of barbed wire. Workmen rolled the barbed wire across the streets to mark the border.

It was warm and sunny on 15 August 1961. Conrad was feeling very hot. That morning he had an argument with a friend.

Conrad began to drink too much. He felt unhappy and confused.

Conrad's parents were poor farmers in the communist German Democratic Republic. They had a flock of sheep.

While his commander was looking the other way Conrad jumped the fence.

Conrad committed suicide in 1998 (aged 56).

When Conrad was 18 he was conscripted (like all young East German men) into the army.

Once the fuss died down Conrad found it hard to get a job. He could not afford a flat. He was one of the poor people in West Berlin, not one of the rich. Eventually he got a job making cars on the Audi assembly line in Bavaria.

In 1961 the East German government decided to build a wall across Berlin.

Conrad's parents hoped that he would stay at home and help with the sheep farming.

Conrad became a sergeant and was made a guard on the Berlin border. His job was to stop people escaping, and to chase and shoot them if they tried. The East German government did not put young men from Berlin on guard at the border because too many escaped: they preferred to use young men from the countryside, with no local links, like Conrad.

Conrad went back to East Germany to visit his family, but they disowned him. They thought he was a traitor.

Conrad's first army posting was on the Polish border.

In West Berlin Conrad was treated like a hero. He was on the front page of newspapers all around the world.

In 1961 Conrad was posted to East Berlin, the capital of the German Democratic Republic.

East Berlin was ruled by communist East Germany. West Berlin was ruled by capitalist West Germany.

Conrad Schumann was unhappy living in East Berlin. He thought he would have a better life in West Berlin.

WHAT WAS THE COLD WAR?

Work out the ingredients that make a Cold War

RECIPE: HOW TO MAKE A COLD WAR

● TAKE TWO SUPERPOWERS ...

At the end of the Second World War two great countries were left standing clear of the ruins – the USA and the USSR. They:

◆ were bigger
◆ had more people
◆ had bigger armies

than any other world power. There was no one else to rival them. They were 'superpowers'.

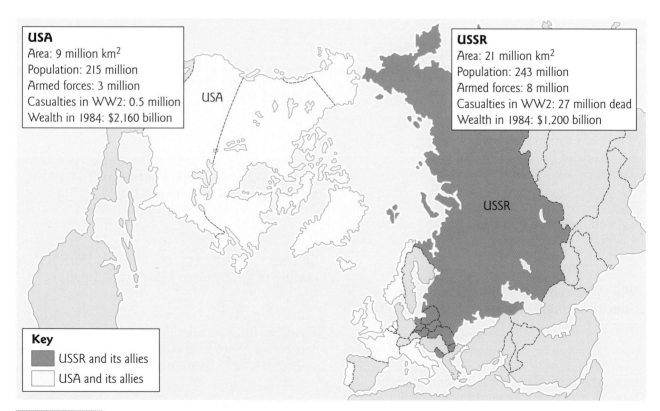

USA
Area: 9 million km^2
Population: 215 million
Armed forces: 3 million
Casualties in WW2: 0.5 million
Wealth in 1984: $2,160 billion

USSR
Area: 21 million km^2
Population: 243 million
Armed forces: 8 million
Casualties in WW2: 27 million dead
Wealth in 1984: $1,200 billion

Key
USSR and its allies
USA and its allies

SOURCE 1 The superpowers compared.

Discuss

Which superpower looks the stronger on paper?

● ... GIVE THEM DIFFERENT UNDERLYING BELIEFS

During the Second World War the USA and USSR had fought together as allies. But they did not really agree with each other. It was only the threat of Hitler that had brought them together. Deep down they had very different beliefs and ideas. The biggest difference was that one believed in capitalism, the other believed in communism. Let's find out what this means.

ACTIVITY

Capitalist or communist?
Here are some features of capitalist and communist systems. Working as a whole class or in groups, your task is to work out which statement applies to which system. You may need to do some research.

◆ There are at least two different political parties to choose between.
◆ A dictatorship: the leaders can do what they want.
◆ There is only one political party.
◆ Individuals own businesses and make profit for themselves.
◆ Business is more efficient.
◆ A democracy: ordinary people choose the government.

◆ The government owns all business. It runs them for the benefit of all.
◆ Business is less efficient.
◆ Some people are very rich, some are very poor.
◆ There is more equality. The state provides housing, education and health care for all.
◆ People can criticise the government.
◆ People can travel anywhere they like.
◆ The government controls all press, TV and radio.
◆ People cannot travel freely.

Discuss
Which system sounds the fairer to you? Why?

USA – CAPITALIST AND DEMOCRATIC

ELECTIONS	INDUSTRY	EQUALITY	FREEDOM

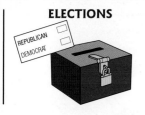 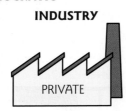 

USSR – COMMUNIST

ELECTIONS	INDUSTRY	EQUALITY	FREEDOM

 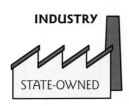 

● ADD SOME SUSPICION AND MISUNDERSTANDING

1 Agreements, 1945

Roosevelt and Stalin, the leaders for most of the Second World War, got on well together. In February 1945, at Yalta, they made plans for how Europe should be governed when Hitler was defeated. Roosevelt agreed (reluctantly) that Eastern Europe would be a Soviet 'sphere of influence'.

2 President Truman drops the bomb, 1945

In April 1945 President Roosevelt died. The new American president, Truman, was much more anti-communist than Roosevelt had been. He was suspicious of Stalin. In May 1945 he ordered the dropping of the first atomic bomb, on Hiroshima in Japan. He made sure the USSR knew about it.

3 Communists take over Eastern Europe

As the USSR freed countries from Hitler's control, instead of withdrawing its troops it left them there. The Soviets then ensured that in each country a communist government took over.

4 A divided Europe
By 1946 the hostility was so great that Winston Churchill spoke of an 'Iron Curtain' across Europe.

5 The Americans help Western Europe, 1947
The Americans sent money called Marshall Aid to help countries in Europe rebuild themselves after the war. However, no aid was given to any country with a communist government.

The USA also paid for British soldiers to fight in Greece to prevent a communist government taking over there.

6 The Berlin Blockade and Airlift, 1948
After the war, both Germany and its old capital Berlin were split between east and west control. West Berlin was in the middle of communist-held East Germany. Stalin tried to force the USA, UK and France to leave West Berlin by blocking all routes into Berlin.

Instead, the Allies flew everything in. For ten months 450 planes a day airlifted supplies into West Berlin. The communist soldiers did not try to shoot down the planes. After ten months Stalin called off the BLOCKADE.

A C T I V I T Y

You are now going to try to see the events of 1945–48 through the eyes of people on both sides. Both sides thought their own actions were quite reasonable but they were very suspicious of everything the other side did. In each of frames 2, 3 and 5 of the story strip there is an empty thought bubble. What might the suspicious observer in each one be thinking? Write some text for the three thought bubbles. Here are some ideas you could use:

◆ This isn't a 'sphere of influence'; it's a take-over!
◆ They are just doing this to threaten us.
◆ They only give money to their supporters.

D I S C U S S

Who seems to be more to blame for the distrust and suspicion – the USA or the USSR? Give your reasons.

7 The Berlin Wall, 1961
Berlin continued to be a point of tension throughout the Cold War. Thirteen years after the Berlin Blockade the USSR built a wall to separate communist East Berlin from capitalist West Berlin. Conrad Schumann (see pages 64–65) was a guard on the Berlin Wall.

● STIR IN GENEROUS AMOUNTS OF PROPAGANDA

Propaganda is information designed to make the person listening to it or seeing it think in a particular way. It is deliberately biased. In war time governments use propaganda to get people on their side. The Cold War was no exception.

SOURCE 2 An American cartoon commenting on Stalin's takeover of Eastern Europe. ▲

ACTIVITY A

Look again at Sources 2 and 3.

1 How have the USA and the USSR been shown in these cartoons?
2 What impression of the USA or the USSR do they give?
3 What is each cartoonist trying to say about the actions of the USA and the USSR?
4 These cartoons are NOT reliable evidence of what the USA or the USSR actually did. However, they are still useful for finding out about the Cold War. How would you use them to tell you about the Cold War?

SOURCE 3 A Russian cartoon commenting on American foreign policy. ▼

● HEAT UP WITH NUCLEAR WEAPONS ... AND SPIES

As soon as the USSR saw the power of the atomic bomb it set its scientists to making one. Soon the two sides were locked in a nuclear arms race to build more and better bombs. Each side used spies to find out what weapons the other side had.

● ... AND SERVE

ACTIVITY B

Your task over the next twelve pages will be to complete your own copy of this table. You should already be able to fill in the first two rows from the work that you have done over the last eight pages.

Ingredient	Example
Beliefs/ideas	
Propaganda	
Arms race	
Suspicion	
Other people's wars	

'THIRTEEN DAYS OF DREAD'
How would you report the news during the Cuban Missile Crisis?

When the first atomic bombs were dropped on Hiroshima and Nagasaki in 1945 no one (not even the Americans who had made them) quite knew what the results would be. Soon, however, it was very clear that these bombs were more deadly than any other weapons in history.

◆ Hundreds of thousands of people were killed in an instant.
◆ Thousands more died a long, lingering death from radiation sickness.
◆ Most of the dead were civilians, not soldiers.

Some people thought these weapons were so deadly they should be banned. But the governments of both the USSR and the USA thought otherwise. Soon there was an arms race between the superpowers:

◆ to build **more** nuclear weapons
◆ to build **more powerful** nuclear weapons
◆ to find **better ways of delivering** the nuclear weapons to their target.

There had been arms races before in history, but, with the invention of the atomic bomb, the arms race of the Cold War became a different, and much more scary, business.

Stage 1: 1945–49
The USSR plays catch-up

The government of the USSR feared that the USA would use one of its atomic bombs against their country very soon, so they were desperate to make their own. With the help of information passed to them by spies, they succeeded in making a bomb in 1949.

Stage 2: 1949–57
Must have more! Must have bigger!

Both sides rushed to build more and bigger weapons. A test explosion of an H-bomb (hydrogen bomb) by the USA in the 1950s took place on a remote island in the Pacific. The cloud was 12 kilometres high in 60 seconds. This bomb was 100 times more powerful than the bombs dropped on Hiroshima and Nagasaki in 1945.

Stage 3: 1957–63
It's not how many you've got, it's where you've got them and how you launch them that counts

◆ In 1957 the USSR developed the first missile that could be launched from the USSR to land in the USA – the ICBM (inter-continental ballistic missile). Soon the USA developed one too.
◆ The USSR launched a satellite into space. It contained only a radio, but the Americans knew that the Soviets could put a hydrogen bomb there too. Soon the USA launched its own satellite into space.
◆ The USA put short-range missiles in Turkey, right on the Soviet border. Soon the USSR did the same in Cuba, 96 kilometres from the USA.
◆ Land-based missiles could be spotted by spy planes. The USA built huge submarines which could launch nuclear missiles. The submarines never stopped in one place long enough to be seen. Soon the USSR did the same. This meant that either side could launch an attack, undetected by the other.

◆ *MAD = Mutually Assured Destruction*

By 1962 both sides had so many nuclear weapons that they would be able to destroy each other many times over. It no longer really mattered which side had more weapons because they both had easily enough to completely obliterate the other.

Some people thought this made the world a safer place. The theory went that neither side would dare launch an attack because they knew the other side would retaliate immediately and they would both be destroyed. This theory was called MAD which stands for Mutually Assured Destruction. Another name was 'nuclear **deterrence**': having your own weapons **put off** the other side from using theirs.

SOURCE 1 US Secretary of Defence Caspar Weinberger explains MAD in *The Times*, August 1982.

If the Soviets knew in advance that a nuclear attack on the USA or our allies would bring swift nuclear retaliation, they would never attack in the first place. They would be deterred from ever beginning a nuclear war.

Others felt that this was a very dangerous state of affairs. The Campaign for Nuclear Disarmament was formed to campaign for governments to get rid of their nuclear weapons voluntarily before they caused awful damage.

The fear was that any small conflict between the superpowers anywhere in the world might escalate and could trigger a nuclear holocaust. All it would take would be one impulsive action or even one mistake, and that would be it – for billions of people living all around the world. Mad indeed!

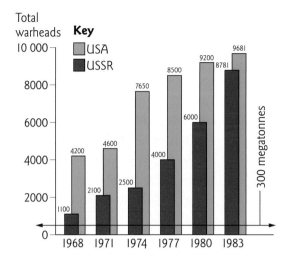

SOURCE 2 A graph showing how the arms race led to the stockpiling of nuclear weapons by both sides. The horizontal line at 300 MEGATONNES is the amount of weapons needed to destroy three-quarters of the people and industry of the USSR or the USA.

ACTIVITY

The governments of the USSR and the USA were spending huge amounts of money on the arms race. They had to justify the cost to their people. Imagine you work for one of the governments at the time. Write some bullet points or sentences that could be used in a propaganda leaflet explaining to your people why they have to pay more tax this year to pay for the nuclear weapons. Here are some notes to help you:

◆ Each side claimed that their missiles were only for defence against the other.
◆ Each insisted they would never be the first to use the weapons.
◆ Each said the other side was hell-bent on war.

You could also look back at the information on page 67 about the initial reasons for the enmity between the USA and the USSR.

SOURCE 3 A cartoon commenting on 'overkill' – the fact that both the USSR and the USA had many times more than enough weapons to destroy the other side.

73

◆ Target Leeds

All this talk about the arms race and the Cold War might seem a little distant. So let's bring things closer to home. Britain was involved too. As a close ally of the USA it had its own nuclear missiles aimed at the USSR and Soviet missiles were targeted at British cities.

So imagine you live in one of the target cities. The labels to the photograph in Source 4 show what would happen if just a 'small' (Hiroshima-sized) bomb were set off 200 metres above City Square in Leeds.

◆ Within one second of the explosion the city centre would be engulfed by a fireball the same temperature as the sun.

◆ Nine seconds later the fireball would have grown to 2700 metres across and would be rising. A crater 65 metres deep and 300 metres across would have formed below the site of the blast.

◆ Ten seconds later a mushroom cloud of debris, dust and steam would be rising to an eventual height of 19 kilometres.

But the blast and the heat are not the end of the destruction. Gradually, over the next six weeks and then over many years, the effects of radiation will be felt. The 'fall-out' – the radioactive dust and debris thrown into the upper air by the mushroom cloud – could well cause more deaths, eventually, than the explosion itself.

SOURCE 4 The possible effects of a nuclear bomb on the Leeds area.

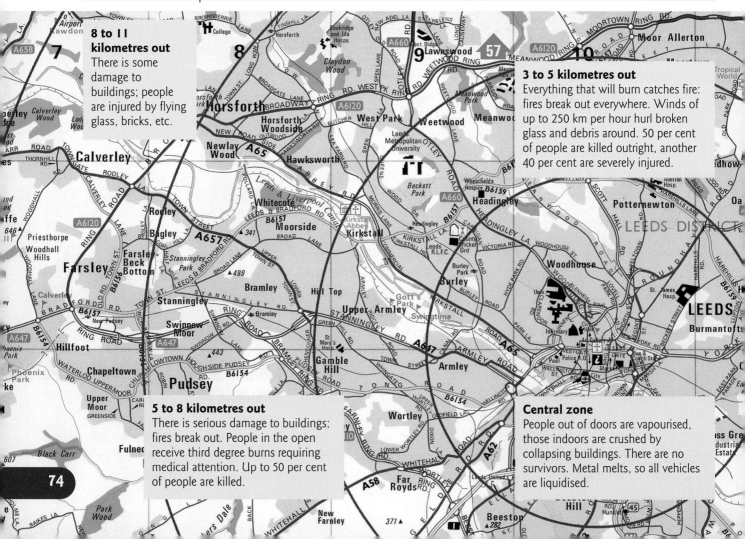

8 to 11 kilometres out
There is some damage to buildings; people are injured by flying glass, bricks, etc.

3 to 5 kilometres out
Everything that will burn catches fire: fires break out everywhere. Winds of up to 250 km per hour hurl broken glass and debris around. 50 per cent of people are killed outright, another 40 per cent are severely injured.

5 to 8 kilometres out
There is serious damage to buildings; fires break out. People in the open receive third degree burns requiring medical attention. Up to 50 per cent of people are killed.

Central zone
People out of doors are vapourised, those indoors are crushed by collapsing buildings. There are no survivors. Metal melts, so all vehicles are liquidised.

Zone 1: Everyone feels severe radiation sickness within a few hours: nausea, vomiting, diarrhoea. This is followed by extreme exhaustion and most people in this zone will be dead within a week.

Zone 2: Most people suffer severe radiation sickness and die within two weeks.

Zone 3: About half die from radiation sickness within two weeks. The rest suffer from a low white blood cell count, so can die from minor infections; also loss of hair, bleeding from gums and genitals, ulcers and fever.

Zone 4: Many people in this zone will survive longer, but are far more likely to get cancer later. Many of the children born after the bomb will be born with a deformity.

SOURCE 5 A map showing the spread of radiation from a 1-megatonne nuclear explosion over Leeds at a time of a gentle north-easterly breeze.

ACTIVITY

Sources 4 and 5 show the effects of just one small nuclear bomb dropped on Leeds. Source 6 shows how Britain would be affected three hours after an attack involving multiple nuclear missiles. It assumes a steady southerly breeze on the day of the attack. Use Sources 4–6 to work out the effects of a nuclear attack on *your* part of Britain.

Now write up your answer as an article for your local newspaper.

DISCUSS

1 'The living would envy the dead.' Do you think this phrase accurately describes the situation after a nuclear attack on Britain?
2 At the same time as, and in response to, the attacks described on these two pages, British or American nuclear missiles would destroy many Soviet cities in the same way. Does that make you feel better, or worse? Explain your feelings.

SOURCE 6 The effects of a nuclear attack on Britain's major cities, air bases and nuclear power stations.

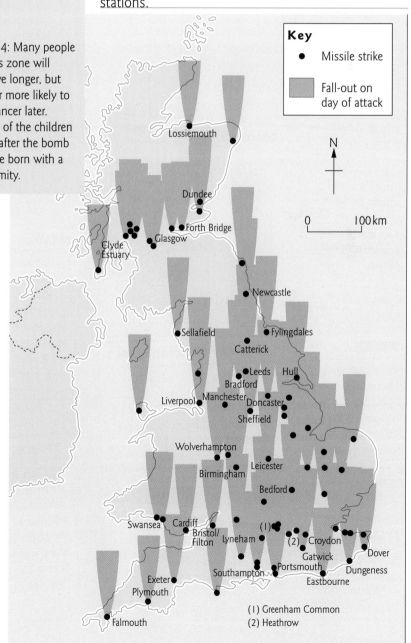

Key
● Missile strike
▨ Fall-out on day of attack

(1) Greenham Common
(2) Heathrow

◆ The Cuban Missile Crisis, 1962

Against the background of the nuclear arms race a dangerous crisis occurred in 1962.

ACTIVITY

In the news room

You work in a news agency in Britain. Sometimes international stories hardly raise any interest but no one is ignoring this particular one. Every day there is a new twist to the tale. People are hungry for news – particularly good news.

Read through the telex messages below (or as you are given them by your teacher). In each case, do a simple analysis of the message before you send it out to the newspapers. Is this good news or bad news and why? Mark each telex with your comments before you send it on.

TELEX **Sunday 14 October 1962**

US spy planes have photographed nuclear missile launchers on Cuba – 60 miles [96 km] off southern coast of USA.

TELEX **Monday 15 October 1962**

Analysis of spy plane photographs reveals launchers *are* Soviet built. Cuba has had communist government for three years. Spies report USSR has been sending military 'advisers' (army officers) and equipment to Cuba for at least a year.

TELEX **Tuesday 16 October 1962**

President Kennedy informed. Experts say missile launchers are *not*, repeat *not*, yet ready to launch missiles. But sites *could* be ready to launch in seven days.

TELEX **Wednesday 17 October 1962**

President Kennedy has set up special committee, ExComm, to advise him. They are considering four options:

1 Invade Cuba
2 Bomb the missile sites – destroy them before they are ready for use
3 Contact USSR. Suggest deal. Soviets remove their missiles from Cuba if USA gets rid of theirs in Turkey
4 Ask the United Nations to help resolve the situation.

ExComm includes 'hawks': heads of armed forces. They are likely to recommend military response – either Option 1 or Option 2.

TELEX **Thursday 18 October 1962**

Soviet ships spotted sailing towards Cuba. Nuclear missiles confirmed *on board*.

Kennedy meets with Soviet Foreign Minister Gromyko. Gromyko insists Soviet aid to Cuba is 'defensive' – he probably doesn't know that USA knows about the missiles on Cuba.

Evening meeting of Excomm is told that some missiles on Cuba are ready to launch.

TELEX **Sunday 21 October 1962**

ExComm has recommended new plan. Instead of attacking Cuba, USA should stop new missiles getting to Cuba. US ships will blockade Cuba. They will search Soviet ships on their way to Cuba and turn them back if they have weapons on board. USSR may regard this as act of war. Kennedy thinks it is worth the risk.

TELEX   **Monday 22 October 1962**

a) Kennedy has appeared on national TV to tell the American people what is happening. He has put armed forces on DefCon Level 3 – just two levels short of all-out war.

b) Soviet leaders expect a US invasion of Cuba. Soviet forces would be outnumbered so their commander is given authority to use nuclear weapons but only on direct order from Moscow.

(later)

c) Panic buying in supermarkets across USA all day.

TELEX   **Tuesday 23 October 1962**

Police reinforcements are rushed to the US embassy in London to battle with 2000 demonstrators. By 10p.m. there are more than 600 police in the square where the embassy is located. Demonstrations against the USA and USSR are also held in Glasgow, Manchester, Bristol, The Hague and Milan.

TELEX   **Wednesday 24 October 1962**

a) Kennedy puts US forces on DefCon Level 2 alert – the first time in the Cold War this has happened.

(later)

b) Robin Mariner, head boy of Midhurst Grammar School in Sussex, leads strike by 40 sixth formers. He sends telegrams to both leaders, Kennedy and Krushchev, calling on them to settle their disagreements peacefully. Explains pupils will not attend school for two days in protest.

TELEX   **Thursday 25 October 1962**

a) US warships stop Soviet ship. This is an act of war. But Soviets do not resist the search. Boat not carrying missiles but oil. Americans let it through to Cuba.

(later)

b) Other Soviet missile-carrying ships have diverted. They are no longer heading towards Cuba.

TELEX   **Friday 26 October 1962**

a) 120,000 US troops and two US aircraft carriers are assembled on the coast of Florida.

(later)

b) In a message to US ExComm that evening, Krushchev offers to remove all missiles from Cuba if USA promises not to invade Cuba.

TELEX   **Saturday 27 October 1962**

a) Krushchev adds new condition: he will only remove missiles if Kennedy also removes US missiles from Turkey. This further demand annoys and depresses ExComm.

b) A US spy plane is shot down over Cuba. The pilot is killed.

c) US Secretary of Defense Robert McNamara is seen strolling in the garden of the White House, smelling the autumn air, looking as if this might be the last time he ever does.

d) US airforce leaders want to bomb Cuba. With difficulty Kennedy dissuades them. His brother Robert (the US Attorney General) suggests ignoring Krushchev's second letter and replying positively to the first. Kennedy agrees and takes this course.

TELEX   **Sunday 28 October 1962**

Khrushchev announces that 'for the sake of world peace' he will remove Soviet missiles from Cuba. Kennedy accepts, orders naval blockade to end.

DISCUSS

'A menace to the human race' or 'A good way of keeping world peace'.
Which of these two statements represents your view of nuclear weapons?

◆ Hot wars

During the 'Cold' War, there were also many 'hot' wars – real conflicts with real fighting and real casualties. The superpower armies never fought each other directly but ...

◆ if it looked as if a capitalist government were under threat from communists the USA set out to defend it. They called this 'containment'. They wanted to stop communism spreading.

◆ when a communist government was being attacked, or even when it was showing signs of following its own policies instead of doing what the USSR wanted, the Soviets would send arms or troops to support the loyal communists.

There are examples of both on this map.

RESEARCH TASK

Do your own research to add information to your own copy of this map.

1 Start with Vietnam. Investigate this topic to decide whether the USA or the USSR succeeded in its aim.

2 Then take the two empty boxes: Hungary and Chile. Find out who intervened here, why and with what results.

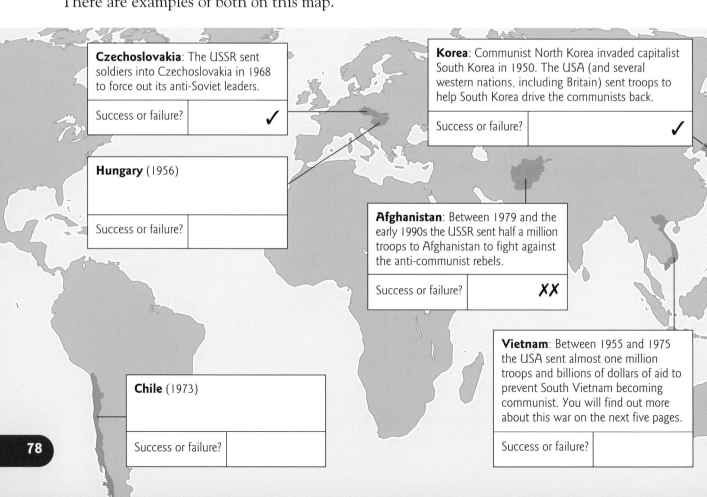

Czechoslovakia: The USSR sent soldiers into Czechoslovakia in 1968 to force out its anti-Soviet leaders.

Success or failure? ✓

Korea: Communist North Korea invaded capitalist South Korea in 1950. The USA (and several western nations, including Britain) sent troops to help South Korea drive the communists back.

Success or failure? ✓

Hungary (1956)

Success or failure?

Afghanistan: Between 1979 and the early 1990s the USSR sent half a million troops to Afghanistan to fight against the anti-communist rebels.

Success or failure? XX

Vietnam: Between 1955 and 1975 the USA sent almost one million troops and billions of dollars of aid to prevent South Vietnam becoming communist. You will find out more about this war on the next five pages.

Success or failure?

Chile (1973)

Success or failure?

◆ *Why did the USA get involved in Vietnam?*

Since 1954 Vietnam had been a divided country. North Vietnam was communist; the South was not. In the 1960s it looked to the Americans as if South Vietnam were about to fall to the communists. They had feared this for years and had been sending money and advisers to prop up the unpopular anti-communist government in the South. They feared that if Vietnam became communist other neighbouring countries would fall to communism, like dominoes.

In 1963 the USA decided money and advisers were not enough. For the first time they sent in combat soldiers. By 1967 there were more than half a million troops in Vietnam.

The timeline below summarises the main events in the Vietnam War.

ACTIVITY A

Many films have been made about the Vietnam War, but filmgoers still seem interested. There may be room for one more film. You are going to be asked to present a proposal to a film studio's commissioning committee (the rest of the class) for a new film. On the next four pages are four possible scenarios. Read through these carefully. They don't tell you all you need to know. You will need to do some more research. Your teacher may give you an additional information sheet about each topic.

Pick the scenario that you think will make the best film. Or if you don't like our choices, research your own.

Then, for your film, write:

a) a title

b) one paragraph about why you chose this story

c) some bullet points about how you would like to finish off this story

d) a comment on how your film will portray the war: is it a heroic struggle between communism and capitalism; a pointless feud which claims millions of innocent lives; a chaotic mistake; or something else?

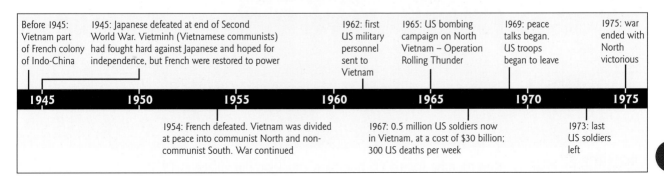

| Before 1945: Vietnam part of French colony of Indo-China | 1945: Japanese defeated at end of Second World War. Vietminh (Vietnamese communists) had fought hard against Japanese and hoped for independence, but French were restored to power | | 1962: first US military personnel sent to Vietnam | 1965: US bombing campaign on North Vietnam – Operation Rolling Thunder | 1969: peace talks began. US troops began to leave | 1975: war ended with North victorious |

1945 — **1950** — **1955** — **1960** — **1965** — **1970** — **1975**

| | 1954: French defeated. Vietnam was divided at peace into communist North and non-communist South. War continued | 1967: 0.5 million US soldiers now in Vietnam, at a cost of $30 billion; 300 US deaths per week | 1973: last US soldiers left |

◆ *The civilian's story*

Phan Thi Kim is the star of this film. She was born in 1963, in the village of Trang Bang in South Vietnam.

🎞 The film starts in 1972. Kim is nine years old. Trang Bang has been attacked before. Villagers have been killed: sometimes by Viet Cong (communist GUERRILLAS); sometimes by the Americans. The village is caught in the middle of a war that just seems to go on for ever.

Now there is talk of new weapons being used. The word is passed around the village. There is a new kind of air raid: US planes sweep over the rainforest spraying it with a very strong and highly toxic weedkiller called Agent Orange. The forest and the farmland around it dies. The Americans are trying to destroy the Viet Cong hideouts but they are killing the land and the people too.

🎞 But there is another, more dangerous, weapon: napalm (pronounced nay-palm). This is like jelly – it sticks to human skin and burns it like acid. The Americans, and their South Vietnamese allies, have been dropping napalm bombs on villages where they think Viet Cong are hiding.

SOURCE 1 A map showing the location of Trang Bang.

One night in June 1972 Kim and her family hear planes overhead. They rush to the Buddhist temple to shelter but the bombs fall directly onto the temple. Kim is covered with napalm. She tears her burning clothes from her body and runs away from the temple, but she is already badly burned on the back of her arms and body.

🎞 What happens next?

SOURCE 2 Phan Thi Kim running from a US bombing attack on her village in 1972.

◆ *The guerrilla's story*

Boy is the star of this film. He is a Viet Cong.

SOURCE 3

This Viet Cong propaganda poster shows guerrillas waiting to ambush US soldiers.

▯ Start with Boy's birth. As he is born his village is being bombed. From his first breath he is surrounded by the sound and suffering of war. The first few minutes of the film fast forward through his childhood birthdays. They show that war is a constant part of his life.

▯ The main action takes place when Boy is 14. A visitor called Chiang arrives in Boy's village. Chiang is a guerrilla. He wants to recruit all the local children to become guerrillas fighting against the Americans. Chiang is a communist. He teaches Boy about communism. 'All are equal. All should work for the common good. The Americans just want to exploit us and keep us poor, like the French and Japanese did before them. Vietnam must be free.' Boy is converted. He becomes the star pupil.

▯ Chiang teaches Boy about guerrilla warfare. 'Learn these principles,' he says:

◆ 'The enemy attacks, we retreat; the enemy camps, we raid; the enemy tires, we attack; the enemy retreats, we pursue.'

◆ 'Never settle in one place. Use surprise attacks and ambushes on small groups of enemy soldiers. Pick them off one by one. Sap the enemy morale. Wear the enemy out.'

◆ 'Wear ordinary clothes. Look like an ordinary villager. If the enemy come looking for guerrillas they will not find you.'

▯ Chiang takes Boy and his friends on their first guerrilla mission. They ambush some American soldiers in the jungle and kill them all. Boy loots one of the dead soldier's possessions. He finds photos of the soldier's girlfriend. Chiang can see that Boy feels sad – but tells him that if he loses his nerve Chiang will have to kill him. 'We must learn to be hard-hearted if the communists are to win this war.'

▯ The main part of the film then follows Boy on his first mission without Chiang. Just he and his friends from the village. They have to ambush some soldiers who are out looking for Viet Cong ...

▣ What happens next?

◆ *The GI's story*

Winston is the star of this film.

🎞 The film starts on the night before Winston leaves for the army. He is only just out of school but the US government has drafted him into the army as a GI (a soldier). He has no choice – if he refuses to be drafted he will go to prison.

🎞 He is having a farewell dinner with his parents and girlfriend. The table is piled high with food but no one is eating. The atmosphere is tense. Winston's parents say how proud they are that he is serving his country. They recall the Second World War and the heroic battle against Hitler. They say that the battle against communism is just as important.

🎞 Then Winston goes off to training camp and he hears a different story. Every GI has his own version.

🎞 So Winston leaves for Vietnam with very mixed feelings. Is he setting off on a heroic struggle like his parents said, or on a mistaken crusade like the other recruits were saying …?

❓ What happens next?

My brother went to Vietnam and he came back a drug addict. My friend took part in a massacre. They just went into the village and killed everyone.

It's real scary, man! You go out on these patrols and any moment someone might ambush you.

My uncle's been there for years. He says we can't win this war. No way. We are fighting to protect the Vietnamese from communism, but they don't want to be protected from it. It's ridiculous.

SOURCE 4   A father wrote to his local newspaper in March 1967:

To the Editor
Here are portions of a letter I have received from my son who is stationed in Vietnam.
Needless to say, I was very much disturbed to read this letter. I think the American people should understand what they mean when they say we should be increasing our war effort in Vietnam.
A GI's Dad.

Dear Mom and Dad,
Today we went on a mission and I am not very proud of myself, my friends or my country. We burnt every hut in sight. I saw a soldier throw a hand-grenade into a hut. After he threw it and was running for cover, we all heard a baby crying from inside the hut. There was nothing we could do. After the explosion we found the mother, two children and an almost new-born baby. The children's fragile bodies were torn apart … Well, Dad, you wanted to know what it was like here; does it give you an idea?
Your son.

◆ *The President's story*

President Lyndon B. Johnson (LBJ) is the star of this film. It's 1968. The President has a big decision to make – whether or not to seek re-election.

SOURCE 5
US President Lyndon B. Johnson.

SOURCE 6 Washington, D.C. 1967: anti-Vietnam war protestors display a sign referring to the President as a war criminal

🎬 The film starts with President Johnson watching television news – there is a report of an anti-Vietnam war protest. Tens of thousands of students are chanting 'LBJ, LBJ. How many kids did you kill today?'

🎬 Later LBJ calls a meeting of his advisers. 'Tell me the worst', he says. And they do ...

🎬 Later LBJ is talking through his problems with his wife – known as the First Lady.

> You must stick with it. If it was right to go into Vietnam then it must be right to see it through to the end. You must resist communism however hard it may seem. Stay committed and the American people will follow.

> This war is costing us $30 billion a year.

> It's costing us 300 young US lives a week.

> It's costing 2000 Vietnamese lives a week.

> We are no closer to winning than when we started.

> We are making communism more popular, not less popular.

> Ex-soldiers are joining in anti-war demonstrations. These are some of the biggest protests in American history.

Then the killer comment: 'And they blame it all on you. No one will vote for you unless you pull the USA out of Vietnam.'

❓ What happens next? What does the President decide?

Forty years after the end of the Second World War the USA and the USSR were still at each other's throats. They each had huge arsenals of terrifying nuclear weapons. Talks between the two to try to cut down the number of weapons repeatedly broke down: neither side trusted the other. US President Ronald Reagan, who was elected in 1980, called the USSR 'the evil empire'. He began a new arms race, with new and enormously expensive weapons: the USA spent a trillion dollars a year on them. Perhaps Reagan intended to break the USSR once and for all by out-spending it.

Then, suddenly, 40 years of Cold War attitudes faded away with the arrival of a new leader in the USSR in 1985: Mikhail Gorbachev.

The last three Soviet leaders had been old men of at least 70. Gorbachev was much younger by comparison, only 54. He was charming, intelligent, with an equally charming and intelligent wife, Raisa. He could see that the USSR was in a terrible mess and was determined to bring about huge changes. He faced up to facts that his predecessors had preferred to sweep under the carpet.

The standard of living of the Soviet people is far lower than in the West. Even though the USSR is rich in fertile land, we can't get food into the shops. We can put an astronaut into space, but we can't make a decent fridge. This is getting worse, not better.

We are spending billions each year on a war in Afghanistan that we can't win.

There is no freedom of speech, so there is no discussion of any of these problems. Managers are not free to manage, they just have to do what we here in Moscow tell them.

Alcoholism is widespread. The life expectancy of Soviet men is actually falling – from 67 in 1964 to 62 in 1980, mainly because of alcohol addiction.

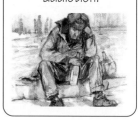

We are ruining our environment. The Aral Sea is disappearing because we have diverted the rivers that feed it. The nuclear power station accident at Chernobyl spread radiation thousands of kilometres. Our rivers are polluted. The air in our industrial cities is dangerous to breathe.

The arms race is taking 25 per cent of the USSR's resources – money we can't afford – yet we still lag behind the USA.

GORBACHEV'S ACTIONS

Gorbachev met US President Reagan in 1986 in Reykjavik, Iceland. He suggested an end to the Cold War. All previous negotiations had fallen down because neither side was prepared to give more than the other. Gorbachev broke with this. He said the USSR would get rid of 3000 missiles in Europe if the USA got rid of just 800. Reagan was strongly anti-communist, but could not be seen to be more warlike than Gorbachev and so he agreed to this deal. The following year the two leaders agreed to remove *all* nuclear weapons from Europe. More agreements over long-range missiles followed.

Gorbachev set out to change the USSR with two key ideas: GLASNOST and PERESTROIKA.

Glasnost means openness. Gorbachev called for free discussion of government policy and the problems facing the USSR. This meant free speech, relaxation of centuries of censorship and free elections with more political parties.

Perestroika means reconstruction. For the first time since communists took over Russia in 1917 people could legally buy and sell things for a profit. Perestroika meant making things that people wanted, at a price which reflected what they cost to make and how much people wanted them, not what the government said the price should be. In other words, a free market.

The war in Afghanistan was ended and Soviet troops brought home.

That was not the end of Gorbachev's whirlwind changes. He could see that Eastern Europe was no longer essential to the security of the USSR. The 'buffer' it provided was useless in a nuclear age. And propping up unpopular governments in Eastern Europe was just a drain on resources. In 1989 he told the people of Eastern Europe that they were free to go their own way. One by one the communist parties in Hungary, Poland, East Germany, Czechoslovakia, Bulgaria and Romania were thrown out, some peacefully, some violently. In November 1989 the Berlin Wall was smashed down and in 1990 East and West Germany were re-united.

SOURCE 1 Gorbachev said later, in 1992:

I knew that an immense task was in front of me. Exhausted by the arms race, the country was at the end of its strength. The economy was getting worse and worse. Developments in science and technology were slow because they were in the hands of government officials. The people's standard of living was declining. Corruption was increasing. We had to reform.

ACTIVITY

On your own copy of the diagram of Gorbachev's problems add a label to each one explaining how Gorbachev tried to solve each problem.

◆ *Success or failure?*

In the West, Gorbachev was treated like a hero. When he visited the USA and Britain he was mobbed by adoring crowds. In Eastern Europe, most people celebrated freedom from Soviet control. The crowds chanted Gorbachev's name as they demolished the Berlin Wall.

In the USSR, however, it was a different story. Gorbachev's policies there did not work. His reforms produced rising prices, falling wages, unemployment, crime and black markets.

Then the USSR itself fell apart. Each of the fifteen republics demanded independence from Russia. Gorbachev was against this. He wanted the Soviet Union to stay together. He sent troops to prevent the republics breaking away but it was too late. The movement that he had started could not be stopped.

On Christmas Day 1991 Gorbachev announced the end of the Soviet Union. Then in 1992 he was forced to resign.

ACTIVITY

On your own copy of the diagram below, add two more labels to the dominoes in each row in order to arrive at the different interpretations of Gorbachev.

SUCCESS

FAILURE

END OF AFGHAN WAR

FREE SPEECH

CRIME

LOW WAGES

REVIEW ACTIVITY A

Why was the Cold War significant?

We're at Significance Alley again. You first came here on page 4. Each of the skittles represents a criterion for significance. Your task is to use what you have found out about the Cold War to see which skittles it knocks down. To show that the Cold War knocks down a skittle you will need to find evidence that it meets this criterion.

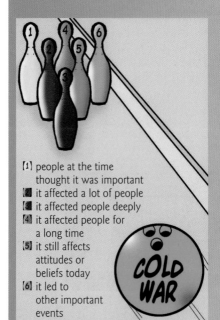

[1] people at the time thought it was important
[2] it affected a lot of people
[3] it affected people deeply
[4] it affected people for a long time
[5] it still affects attitudes or beliefs today
[6] it led to other important events

You will probably have done this activity twice before so you will know just what to do. Working with a partner or in a group, write down all the evidence you can think of from pages 64–86 that would hit any of the skittles. You don't need to sort your evidence to start with, just brainstorm your ideas. Write each one on a separate piece of paper or card.

Now take a large piece of paper. Draw and label the skittles, then move each of your cards next to the skittle it fits with. The more evidence you can add the better. If you have only a little evidence maybe the skittle will just wobble. If you have lots of evidence it should send the skittle flying. If you have none at all the skittle will be untouched.

When you have finished, note which of the six skittles fell, which wobbled and which stayed upright. Was this more of a strike or less of a strike than the Great War and the Second World War?

REVIEW ACTIVITY B

Here is another familiar activity. Your challenge is to prepare a PowerPoint presentation which uses just three slides. Each slide should carry a Cold War fact that you think everyone should know. One way of working would be to start with a list of up to ten facts and then cut these down to the most important three. Work in groups if you prefer. You can use a maximum of 25 words on each slide. Prepare a commentary to go with each slide explaining *why* this is an important fact for people to know about the Cold War.

REVIEW ACTIVITY C

Complete a copy of this diagram.

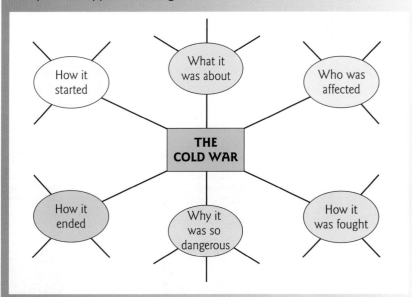

Then, on your completed diagram, highlight in one colour aspects of the Cold War that are similar to the two world wars. In another colour highlight the aspects that are different.

CONCLUSION
WAS THERE MORE TO THE TWENTIETH CENTURY THAN WAR?

MOLLIE SIMPSON'S CENTURY

I liked school well enough. Everyone stayed until they were at least 11. I stayed until I was 13 because I was quite bright.

I got £2 per week. A fortune! I spent my first wages on some new shoes and a pretty hat.

First day at school, 1905

First job, 1913

So many young men got killed in the Great War: there were not many to go round us girls. Still, I was a lucky one. Lewis and I went to Wales for our honeymoon. I'd never been so far from home before. Because my Dad was station master he got us cheap tickets in the best carriages.

Every Friday we went to the cinema. It was like a palace inside. There was always a newsreel, a B picture and then the Main Feature. My two sons liked Hollywood westerns, but my daughter Norah liked the romances: she cut pictures of the stars out of film magazines and stuck them over her bed.

Honeymoon, 1921

Out to the Odeon, 1937

Wartime. My three children,
Donald, John and Norah, 1942

John was the first person in his street to get a telly. It was only black and white.
We all used to go round there to watch anything special. Tellies were so expensive and unreliable that most people rented.

First TV, 1955

War again! Donald was captured in Malaya by the Japanese. We didn't know if he was dead or alive for three years. He never recovered from what he'd been through. He was always getting ill. He died of the flu in 1955.
John was the hero, I suppose, with his two medals. He was always the lucky one.
Even Norah had to join up.

I'd never done anything like this before but I'd had enough of war in my lifetime.
I was dead against nuclear weapons. My legs weren't good but I wanted to go on the march so my friend pushed me in my wheelchair.

John persuaded us to go to Spain. I never thought I would do that. Only rich people went abroad before. But now even we could afford it with these new package tours.
I loved the view from the plane, and the warm sea, and sitting out with a drink in the evenings in just a summer dress.

First trip abroad, 1963

First political demonstration, 1981

ACTIVITY A

1 Do you remember the criteria on the skittles in Significance Alley? Use the criteria to decide which event in Mollie's life affected her:

   a) most deeply
   b) for the longest time.

2 How did each of the following *factors* affect Mollie's life?

   ◆ Technology
   ◆ Entertainment
   ◆ Transport
   ◆ War.

3 Does Mollie's life story suggest that the events listed in the National Curriculum (which you have studied in this book) were the most important events of the twentieth century?

Some sad times. Some happy ones. It's hard to say which was the most important.

◆ *What should the twentieth century be remembered for?*

Different people have different answers to this question. This book has been written for the National Curriculum so it deals with the topics the government thought were significant: the two World Wars, the Holocaust and the Cold War.

On pages 88 and 89 you saw that an old person, who had lived through the twentieth century, might have their own view about what had been most important. Other people in other countries would have their own ideas.

Now that we've reached the last two pages, what does the author of this book think?

I think the events listed in the National Curriculum were significant, because, as I have tried to show you, millions of ordinary people's lives were blasted apart by them. But I think they are not the only things that the twentieth century should be remembered for. Here are some others.

The end of European empires

After three or four hundred years of being ruled by foreign powers, people all over the world threw off colonial rule.

Space travel

Human beings left our planet and travelled into space for the first time ever.

DISCUSS

What do *you* think the twentieth century should be remembered for?

1 Look at the suggestions given here. Add any ideas of your own which you think have been missed.
2 Divide the ideas into the following groups.

   a) Which are in the National Curriculum, which are not?
   b) Which apply only to Britain; which apply to the whole world?
   c) Which affect governments; which affect ordinary people?

3 Reach your own decision about which of these many ideas the twentieth century should be remembered for most of all. It could be one of the topics you have studied in this book or it could be something else. Explain your choice to the rest of the class.

Globalism

Differences between people all over the world have been broken down. Around the world now you can find people playing football – even supporting the same teams; queuing up for the same kind of burgers; wanting to wear the same make of trainers.

The changing role of women

The twentieth century changed women's lives. For the first time in history women in many countries are getting near to equality.

WHAT SHOULD THE TWENTIETH CENTURY BE REMEMBERED FOR?

The rise of the USA

The twentieth century ended with one country almost 'controlling the world' – the USA. This has never happened in history before.

TV and the internet

These things have utterly changed people's lives. We can find out about events anywhere in the world and see them in our own homes within hours.

Air travel

You can get to anywhere in the world in 24 hours.

◆ Glossary

ALLIANCE an agreement between countries to help each other, particularly if one gets involved in a war

ANTIBIOTIC a drug which kills harmful bacteria

APARTHEID a system of racial separation and white rule in South Africa from 1948 to 1994

APPRENTICE a young person who is learning a trade or skill by working alongside a qualified person

ARMISTICE a cease-fire in a war

ARMS RACE a race between two or more countries to build more or better weapons than the other

ARYAN a word used by the Nazis for the German 'race'

ASSASSINATE to murder for political reasons

ATOMIC FISSION the splitting of the nucleus of an atom into two roughly equal parts accompanied by an enormous release of energy

BATTALION a large number of soldiers, part of a regiment

BIASED one-sided, partial

BLOCKADE cutting off all access to a town or country

CAPITALIST describes an economic system in which individuals own and run businesses for their own profit

COMMUNIST describes an economic system, proposed initially by Karl Marx, in which the state owns all forms of business and runs them for the benefit of all citizens

CONSCRIPTION compulsory military service

EMPIRE a number of countries and peoples all ruled by one power

EPIDEMIC a disease affecting lots of people at the same time

FRONT LINE the foremost position of an army, nearest to the enemy

GARRISON the military force holding a fort or town

GLASNOST Russian word meaning 'openness' – more democracy, free speech (see also perestroika)

GUERRILLA a fighter who uses unorthodox methods of fighting, for example, hiding from the enemy, making sudden attacks and then hiding again

LIFE EXPECTANCY how long you can expect to live; the average life span

MEGATONNE a way of measuring the strength of a nuclear bomb, equal to a million tonnes of an ordinary explosive such as TNT

PERESTROIKA a Russian word meaning re-structuring – bringing more freedom into the Russian communist economy (see also glasnost)

PUTSCH a German word for an attempt to seize power by force

RADIATION radioactive particles given off by a nuclear reaction or explosion

RECEPTION CENTRE an office set up during the Blitz on British cities in the Second World War where homeless people could go

REPARATIONS money paid by Germany after the First World War to the victorious Allies as compensation for the damage caused by the war

SNIPER a rifleman who fires from a concealed place at enemy individuals

SOCIALIST someone who wants an economic system in which the state controls all kinds of business activity for the equal benefit of all citizens

◆ Index

THIS IS HISTORY!

◆ Titles in the series

Pupil's Books (PB) and Teacher's Resource Books (TRB) are available for all titles.

Write Your Own Roman Story	PB 0 7195 7717 9	TRB 0 7195 7718 7
The Norman Conquest	PB 0 7195 8555 4	TRB 0 7195 8556 2
King John	PB 0 7195 8539 2	TRB 0 7195 8540 6
Lost in Time	PB 0 7195 8557 0	TRB 0 7195 8558 9
'King' Cromwell?	PB 0 7195 8559 7	TRB 0 7195 8560 0
The Impact of Empire	PB 0 7195 8561 9	TRB 0 7195 8562 7
Dying for the Vote	PB 0 7195 8563 5	TRB 0 7195 8564 3
The Trenches	PB 0 7195 8565 1	TRB 0 7195 8566 X
The Holocaust	PB 0 7195 7709 8	TRB 0 7195 7710 1
The Twentieth Century	PB 0 7195 7711 X	TRB 0 7195 7712 8

◆ Acknowledgements

Written sources
pp.32–33 from *What's It All About* by Michael Caine, published by Century. Reprinted by permission of The Random House Group Ltd; **p.49** from *Hiroshima* by John Hersey (Penguin Books 1946) copyright © John Hersey 1946, 1973, 1985.

Photographs
Cover *l* Imperial War Museum, London, *c* Hulton Archive, *r* SPL; **p.2** *t* Michael Holford, *br* The British Library, *bl* People's History Museum, Manchester, *bc* Time Life Pictures/Getty Images; **p.5** PCL/Alamy; **p.8** courtesy Mr D.R.P. Ferriday; **p.12** *l* Hulton Archive, *r* Topham Picturepoint; **p.13** *l* & *r* © Bettmann/Corbis; **p.15** Imperial War Museum, London; **p.16** Imperial War Museum, London; **p.17** courtesy Mrs Ellen Walters; **p.19** *t* Reproduced with the permission of the Library Committee of the Religious Society of Friends, *b* Imperial War Museum, London; **p.20** TopFoto/Fotomas; **p.21** Imperial War Museum, London (Q30876); **p.25** *r* SV-Bilderdienst, *l* © NI Syndication; **p.28** Fox Photos/Hulton Archive; **p.31** Nordicphotos/Alamy; **p.33** *t* Imperial War Museum, London, *b* Popperfoto.com; **p.36** © Bristol United Press; **p.37** © Bristol United Press; **p.38** Hulton Archive; **p.39** *tl* Hulton Archive, *bl* Imperial War Museum, London (ZZZ9182C), *r* © Bristol United Press; **p.40** Popperfoto.com; **p.41** Hulton Archive; **p.42** TopFoto; **p.43** *tl* Associated Press/U.S. Navy, *tr* & *b* Hulton Archive; **p.44** Imperial War Museum, London (A15365); **p.45** *t* courtesy Ian Dawson, *b* from *We Also Served: Mahinder Singh Pujji*, A Memorial Gates Project (BASS Publications, Birmingham); **p.46** Imperial War Museum, London (OEM3606); **p.48** Hulton Archive; **p.49** Associated Press/Corps of Engineers; **p.51** *t* Associated Newspapers/Solo Syndication, *bl* © Hulton-Deutsch Collection/Corbis, *br* Hulton Archive; **p.52** © Corbis; **p.53** AKG Images; **p.54** *t* Yad Vashem Film and Photo Archive, *b* Willy Georg/Rex Features; **p.55** Imperial War Museum, London (HU86369); **p.56** *t* Yad Vashem Film and Photo Archive, *b* AKG Images; **p.57** Photo courtesy Jack Kagan; **p.58** *t* TopFoto, *bl* © Ullstein/Keystone Pressedienst, *br* Hulton Archive; **p.59** *tl* © Langevin Jacques/Corbis Sygma, *tr* Popperfoto.com, *b* Hulton Archive; **p.60** Imperial War Museum, London; **p.63** John Cole/Alamy; **p.64** TopFoto/AP; **p.70** *b* © Krokodil; **p.73** © Telegraph Group Limited 1967; **p.74** © Collins Bartholomew Ltd 2004 Reproduced by Permission of HarperCollins Publishers www.collinsbartholomew.com; **p.79** *l* & *r* Moviestore Collection; **p.80** Associated Press/Nick Ut; **p.81** TopFoto; **p.83** *l* Popperfoto.com, *r* © Bettmann/Corbis; **p.84** © Peter Turnley/Corbis ; **p.85** *tl* © Roger Ressmeyer/Corbis, *tc* © Peter Turnley/Corbis, *tr* © Bernard Bisson/Corbis Sygma, *bl* TopFoto/AP, *br* © Gilles Peress/Magnum.

(*t* = top, *b* = bottom, *l* = left, *r* = right, *c* = centre)

Every effort has been made to trace all copyright holders but if any have been inadvertently overlooked, the Publishers will be pleased to make the necessary arrangements at the first opportunity.